MAGNIFICENT MILE:
A History of Hillsboro Beach

by

Carmen Racine McGarry

Magnificent Mile: A History of Hillsboro Beach
by Carmen R. McGarry

Published by RitAmelia Press
7651 SE 118 Avenue
Morriston FL 32668-4843
Printed in the United States of America

ISBN: 0-9641216-3-8
Library of Congress No.: Pending at Release Date

Cataloging in Publication data

McGarry, Carmen R. 1941-
Magnificent Mile: a History of Hillsboro Beach by Carmen R. McGarry
p. cm.
Includes bibliographical references and photographs
ISBN 0-9641216-3-8 (hard cover):
1. Florida--History. 2. Hillsboro Beach (Broward County, Fla.)--History. I. Title
975.935--dc20 CIP

CIP provided in cooperation with A+ Writing.

Jacket photographs by Carmen R. McGarry
Jacket Design by Barbara G. Moss

To the memory of my dear friend
Lenora Marie Rosch

Contents

Preface

The development of Hillsboro Beach was gradual; there were no booms or busts as the area metamorphosed from swamp to bustling town. Bad times, rather, were caused by nature and growing pains. No one settled here to start a colony, nor were there any organizations established to record history. There is still only a main street--A1A--and no stop signs, cab stands or sidewalks.

Through the years it has been known by varying descriptive names, such as "Millionaire's Mile," "Private Sandbox to a Privileged Few," and "Easy Street." Today, it is frequently labeled simply "The Mile."

Located on an island north of the Hillsboro Inlet, Hillsboro Beach stretches about 3.2 miles from Pompano Beach to Deerfield Beach. With the Atlantic Ocean to the east and the Intracoastal Waterway to the west, at its widest point it is approximately 900 feet wide.

Its beaches are private, and for many years it has enjoyed an exclusiveness seldom seen elsewhere. The lighthouse at the inlet is dated at the turn of the century and is one of the best preserved historic sites in the state, yet it is frequently ignored and unlisted as a tourist attraction. Next to it is one of the first exclusive clubs in Florida, one which has catered to dignitaries and aristocrats from around the world. As one of the nation's best kept secrets, the inlet is frequently left off maps of Florida, even though it has proven to be a very important egress and ingress for the state's waterways and has held a front row seat throughout Florida's development.

In *Magnificent Mile: A History of Hillsboro Beach*, I have tried to describe the development of this town from swamp to today's choice community. This book, I believe, responds to a growing interest in history and preservation in general and a curiosity about local history in particular. My purpose is to show the historical wealth claimed by "The Mile." People from varying backgrounds and with a broad range of goals have made this area what it is today; their stories deserve to be told.

As late as the beginning of the 20th century, the area was still largely uninhabited, a wilderness of swamp and scrub. However, with the development of the railroad, the automobile, the telephone and electricity, Hillsboro became a permanent residence for many prominent families. For whatever reason these people came, from many parts of the world, they chose to build their homes here. Their diverse backgrounds offered a potpourri of knowledge and talent to the community.

These pioneers brought a wealth of talent and wanderlust, and many who were not monetarily wealthy when they arrived became so as they pursued their dreams. Collectively they developed "The Mile" and left a legacy which we cherish today.

Research for this book took me as far afield as Australia, Europe, upstate New York and the National Archives, as well as to local historical societies, libraries, courthouses and individuals willing to share their memories with me through interviews. Sometimes hours were spent gleaning but one small piece of information. Yet such items--perhaps the trivia of yesterday--are significant within the framework of a subjective history. This, then, is one aspect of writing a history: one tidbit at a time.

Any history is defined by the elements thought by the author to be interesting enough to bear repeating. It has been my intention to capture the richness of the web of life in Hillsboro Beach, highlighting people who came here full of purpose, making the town what it is today through the influence of surrounding communities.

Skillful artisans, architects and builders created homes, apartment buildings, restaurants and hotels. Those who came with riches helped found the town, but wealth of spirit was even more important. Those who recognized the potential of the area went to extremes to protect the secluded nature of the place, offering respect for the privacy of world leaders, aristocrats and titans of the corporate world.

A letter dated June 21, 1977, describes the attitude that had developed over the years. On letterhead announcing "TOWN OF Hillsboro Beach," it was addressed to The Barefoot Mailman Hotel at 1061 Hillsboro Beach, Pompano Beach, Florida 33062. The message comes quickly to the point:

Gentlemen:

One of our commissioners brought to my attention your advertisement of June 16, 1977 in The Weekly Herald in which you draw attention to what you call "ON MILLIONAIRE'S MILE! Hillsboro Beach."

Our Commissioners have consistently taken the position that it should discourage any reference to our area as a specific home for millionaires as there is a danger of drawing attention of the criminal element to the Town.

It is true that we probably have a few millionaires but most of our people are here to enjoy our beach and the sunshine.

We ask that you discontinue the use of this phrase in your advertising.

The communique was signed by Clyde H. Shaffer, Mayor, and copies were distributed to "All Commissioners" and "Attorney Clarke."

The sentiment put so succinctly by Mayor Shaffer is still prevalent today. The title "Magnificent Mile" is more descriptive, for it takes into account much more than monetary wealth. Hillsboro Beach is truly magnificent in its wealth of beauty, ideas, dedication and wherewithal to bring about progress.

Historical writing is more than documents and facts. I have looked beyond the numbers and dates, focusing more on the behavior and interests of the people who made our history. While I have attempted to report events in chronological order within chapters, there is a natural overlapping of years when events and topics refuse to be confined to a straight path.

A significant aspect of this book is its attention to those who have served the town in official capacities. The police force, for example, has played an important role on "The Mile," having accepted the pace set by our first elected mayor and the town marshal. The town has always had a great deal of pride in its police and the care they have given the residents. Administrators also have been dedicated in their service to the community.

The goal of the town leaders has always been to maintain the status-quo and protect the privacy of residents within a framework of natural beauty; the stratagem has been to do this and embrace progress at the same time. This has always been the challenge, to accommodate conflicts without drastic visible change.

Many Hillsboro Beach residents today are retirees who live in fashionable condominiums and homes. These seniors are very active, making sure their needs are met and their voices are heard.

The future of "The Mile" depends on leaders and citizens to find a balance between modern demands for progress and the needs of a natural environment that might be endangered by such improvement. As we prepare to enter the 21st century, we who inhabit "The Mile" are confident that we are an important link in "The Gold Coast," which runs from Palm Beach to Miami--wealthy in history, magnificent in accomplishment.

Acknowledgments

Many have contributed their time, patience and, especially, encouragement toward the success of this history. I owe much gratitude to the following: Tony Gaspero, Judy Wilson, Irene George, Darlene Pfister, Dave Denman, Dan Dodge, Helen Landers, Rodney Dillon, Barbara Poleo, Tom Hassis, Amo Angeletti, Charles Kanode, Dean Lindstrom, Ann Grainger, Barbara Bittner, Chief Ralph Dunn, Lt. Bob Jones and Stuart McIver.

Tallahassee
Jacksonville
St. Augustine
St.
Petersburg
Tampa
Lake
Okeechobee
Palm Beach
Hillsboro Beach
Fort Lauderdale
Miami
Key West

Introduction: An Overview

The town of Hillsboro Beach became a reality in 1939, but centuries of history and millennia of pre-history preceded that date. The name Hillsboro was first attached to this barrier island in 1770 by German cartographer William Gerard DeBrahm, Esq., when he made maps of the area and used the name "Hillsboro Outlet" to refer to what is now known as the Hillsboro Inlet. He described the condition of the inlet as suitable only for boats, meaning that large vessels could not enter because of the shallow water.

We do not know what motivated DeBrahm to honor Lord Wills Hills, the Earl of Hillsborough in the Irish peerage, by putting his name on the map. Although the Earl never set foot in the colonies, more than 20 locations in the United States carry the name Hillsboro or Hillsborough. The earl always gave the most determined opposition to any concessions to America, and he vociferously objected to having any mention of American independence admitted in the House of Lords.

Both men had prestigious government appointments. Hillsborough had been named President of the Board of

Trade and Foreign Plantations in 1763--the year the British wrested control of the peninsula from the Spanish--and a year later DeBrahm was appointed surveyor general of the Southern District, which included South Florida. Later the Earl was named Secretary of State for the Colonies.

When DeBrahm mapped present-day Hillsboro Beach, the island was separated from the Atlantic Coastal Ridge by extensive fresh water streams, as well as fresh and salt water marshes and lagoons. West of the island and the fresh water marshes, the ridge became the focus of pioneer--and later, modern--settlement. Rising about one or two meters above sea level, the ridge is about three miles wide. In the early years the ridge supported a vast pinewood forest, with oak and hardwood hammocks near the edges.

Millions of years earlier, there had been nothing at all. When the Appalachian chain was being formed by relentless glacial formations, the Florida Plateau lay thousands of feet below sea level. The carbonate shells of dead microscopic sea animals built a framework for thick limestone on top of the rocks. Fine sand and clay washed down from the mountains in the north, until finally a dome of land appeared.

Florida was an island at first, 150 feet above the ocean, in the Ocala area. Slowly the strait closed, creating an abbreviated version of our Florida. This short peninsula extended only to the lower rim of the fresh water lake now called Okeechobee.

Other foundations built up around the finger of earth. The deaths of crustaceans added to the land. Wind and waves created sand barriers. Sand on the northwest and coral to the southeast formed more land. The depression in between was the Everglades, where marine life turned into limestone and decaying vegetation was transformed into rich peat and muck beds.

While the Florida peninsula and its barrier islands were coming to life, ice was moving down from the north, destroying the ragged peaks and mountains in its path. By the time the ice reached the area now called Pennsylvania, animals were seeking the warmth and vegetation of the Florida Plateau, the youngest part of the earth.

Camels, one-toed horses, mastodons, elephants and bison traveled south, feeding off the fauna of the newest land. They were followed by mammoths, giant sloths, armadillos, deer, tapirs and peccaries, stripping the last of the vegetation. Preying on the herbivores were wolves, lions, saber-toothed tigers and bears.

Evidence of humans in the region has been dated to the Paleo Indian Period (10,000-8,000 B.C.). Radiocarbon techniques were used to analyze evidence found in southern Dade County in Cutler. This evidence determined that deer and rabbits and some marine fauna were exploited by inhabitants here during that period.

While the glacier had reduced sea levels and increased the size of Florida, the opposite occurred during the Post Glacial Period (or Archaic Period), 6500-1000 B.C.; the sea level rose and greatly diminished Florida's land size. We can be certain that the barrier island now known as Hillsboro Beach was under water. As land emerged once again, cypress swamps and hardwood forests began to develop. This period was characterized by an increased reliance by native populations on shellfish and marine resources, as well as a generally expanded base for hunting, fishing and plant gathering throughout South Florida.

Until recently archaeologists were not aware of the extent and nature of Archaic Period sites in southern Florida. This period is distinguished by the development of fiber-tempered pottery. Some of this pottery, found on Marco Island, has been dated from as early as 3400 B.C.

Indian burial mounds are scattered throughout Florida, including one on the north side of Hillsboro Inlet and another on the south side of Hillsboro River (both discovered in 1974). Indians traveling down the coast would land at the natural inlet and make camp on the east side of the lake, where shellfish were abundant.

Other sites in the vicinity include a burial mound in Pompano, which the city set aside in the 1920's as a park, and a huge site at Jupiter Inlet. The latter is a "shell midden" containing millions of discarded shells. The mound of shells is so large the Jupiter Lighthouse was built on top to give added height. A total of 16 sites were assessed within the northeast Broward area with the May 1993 Archaeological Survey of Northeast Broward County.

When the Europeans arrived here in the 16th century, they encountered a thriving population with at least five separate tribes in southern Florida. They were the Tequesta in the southeast, the Calusa in the southwest, the Jeaga and the Ais along the east coast (north of the Tequesta), and the Mayaimi near Lake Okeechobee. Estimates put the number of Indians in South Florida at that time at 20,000.

This is when written records about life in Florida began. It was 1513 when the Spanish explorer and adventurer Juan Ponce de Leon arrived. He waded ashore on the northeast coast of Florida, possibly near St. Augustine. No firm evidence of other non-natives ever having discovered Florida has been found. Ponce de Leon called the place "La Florida" in honor of *Pascua Florida*, Spain's Easter-time Feast of the Flowers.

The face of Florida changed again when Britain gained control of it in 1763. The British had captured Cuba, during the just-ended Seven Years War, and now they traded the island for the peninsula. Although British rule lasted only twenty years, they did map much of the entire coast. They also worked to develop and maintain good relations with the natives, a previously little-known southward-moving group of Creeks that the British called "Seminolies."

Of the estimated 20,000 Indians present when the Spanish arrived, the native population had been reduced to several hundred when the British took over. Two hundred fifty years of dealing with the white man had taken their toll. Many of the Indians are said to have traveled to Cuba with their Spanish conquerors. An early account and earlier evidence of a Seminole settlement in South Florida is an 1837 description and map by topographer John Lee Williams, who studied the Everglades during the Second Seminole War of 1835-42. Before Williams' study, the region had been a complete mystery to white men.

It was to protect her interests that England proceeded to create more surveys and geographical data. Through the efforts of Samuel Holland, the office of the Surveyor General was established, and DeBrahm was dispatched to the "Southern District."

DeBrahm was a man of great versatility. An engineer and botanist, he had studied many other sciences and was not content to just survey the land. Shortly after his government appointment and arrival here in 1764, he began recording the climate and describing what grew and lived in southern Florida at the time. In 1769 he appointed Bernard Romans to be the principal deputy surveyor for the district. Romans' survey resulted in accurate maps and publication of *A Concise Natural History of East and West Florida*. DeBrahm's descriptions were presented to King George III in the early 1770s.

Although there were many maps of Florida drawn by early surveyors, most were for navigational purposes and few ever ventured beyond the coast.

The first settlements in south Florida were scattered Indian villages and Bahamian fishing communities in the Keys. Other settlers along the Atlantic coast were discouraged by the treachery of submerged reefs and the shallowness of the inlet.

In the early 19th century the U.S. Government lent an encouraging hand. Spain had regained Florida in the settlement which ended the American Revolution, but the United States acquired all of Florida from Spain in 1821. All of the land became the property of the United States, but to honor claims by those who had occupied specific land during Spanish rule, the government conceived the Donation Act of 1824. Under the act, claims were deeded to some of the settlers. In 1825 a parcel known as the "Frankee Lewis Donation" was deeded to a Lewis family. It was located on the New River, in what is today Fort Lauderdale.

Charles Vignoles, a civil and topographical engineer, was one of the first to extensively describe the Hillsboro River, writing his portrayal of the area in the early 1820s. On his map the inlet was called the "Hillsboro, or Middle River Inlet."

After the Swamp and Overflowed Land Act of 1850, Florida joined the union, and unclaimed lands were deeded to the state for internal improvements; funds generated through this transfer were used to dig the Intracoastal Waterway.

Despite the apparent merits of such an important artery, the dredging and accompanying accouterments of the system severely impacted some natural features of the area. All of the fresh water features were ultimately destroyed, so that now the island called Hillsboro Beach has only salt water mangroves and manmade (salt water) canals. Other portions of the old fresh water systems were eventually covered by fill so that homes could be constructed on top.

After Florida became a United States Territory, the federal government built lighthouses, and a U.S. Naval fleet was sent to improve conditions along the coast. In addition, the navy was sent to remove the pirates operating around the Keys, and a naval base was set up in Key West.

In 1841, Lieutenant J.C. Ives, a United States topographical engineer, described the Hillsboro River and the Inlet:

> *. . . the Hillsboro, a stream fifty feet broad, lined with mangroves, and increasing in size to its mouth, five miles distance where it is about a quarter of a mile in width. Hillsboro Inlet runs south for a mile, leaving a ridge of sand three hundred feet wide, between it and the Ocean. It narrows very much towards the entrance, affording a passage for row-boats only, the depth of water on the bar at low tide is about two feet. Five hundred yards from the bar, the river can generally be forded: the water being three feet in depth.*

Florida became the 27th state in 1845, and William D. Moseley was elected governor. Five years later population had swelled to 87,445, which included about 39,000 slaves and 1,000 free blacks. For several years the area remained undeveloped, and no references to the inlet are recorded.

The key to development in South Florida was transportation. The idea of connecting the inland waterways running north and south along the coast was an obvious tactic to further future development. The major obstacle was lack of financing to build such a project and lack of business to support it, once it was completed. In 1850 the federal government passed a law allowing Florida to acquire ownership of the federal "swamp lands" within its territory.

An "Internal Improvement" statute followed in Florida in 1855. Transfer of flooded lands to pay for the improvements to drain the swamp lands and build canals encouraged the work. In 1881 the Florida East Coast Canal Company was formed to connect the lakes and rivers, which eventually became the Intracoastal Waterway, from Jacksonville to Biscayne Bay. The canal was to be fifty feet wide and a minimum of five feet deep. The canal company was to receive 3,840 acres of land for each mile of canal constructed.

When Civil War engulfed the country, Florida was not ravaged as were some other southern states. No decisive battles were fought on Florida soil. The United States gunboat *Sagamore*, on March 8, 1863, captured a small sloop off the coast of Hillsboro. The mission of the *Sagamore* was to blockade the coast and send ashore occasional landing parties to search for and destroy Confederate saltworks and other endeavors. However, no federal troops came ashore at Hillsboro.

In 1884 a United States Coastal and Geodetic Survey party established a camp at the Hillsboro Inlet in order to map the coastline. The expedition, aboard the sloop *Steadfast*, studied the inlet in detail and made many soundings there.

During this time, U.S. mail to and from Hillsboro was carried by men known collectively as The Barefoot Mailman. (See Chapter 2, "The Barefoot Mailman.") Three years after the *Steadfast* expedition was mounted, mail carrier Ed Hamilton disappeared along his route between Lake Worth and the Fort Lauderdale House of Refuge.

South Florida was still undeveloped in the late 1800s; the Everglades were covered by water, as were the rich lands around Lake Okeechobee. On the Atlantic coast, a thin strip of land--composed, primarily, of rock and sand--supported pin and scrub vegetation.

By 1890 there were six families in the area surrounding the Hillsboro River. In 1892 the Bay Biscayne Road was built, and in 1896 the Florida East Coast Railway reached south to the Hillsboro River. The availability of transportation for produce encouraged more people to settle and farm.

Even in the late 1890s the area around the Hillsboro Inlet was still a wilderness. Living was very difficult because of sand, mosquitoes and weather. The shoals and reefs off the coast made shipping very dangerous and prevented access to the land except for very shallow draft boats. Shipwrecks, which had been recorded in this area as early as the 17th century, extended into the early 20th century. (See Chapter 1, "Shipwrecks and Treasure.")

Shortly after the railroad had reached the area, an engineer with the railway, C.C. Hunt, platted twelve acres of land along the river. He named the settlement Hillsborough. One year later, 1898, twenty settlers petitioned Washington for the establishment of a post office. In June 1898, John B. Thomas was appointed as the first postmaster of Deerfield. This station was the only one between Miami and Delray Beach.

Two hotels were established, the Pioneer and the Australian, along with two stores. Although the settlement continued to prosper, the beaches were a wilderness that was used only for picnics and fishing. In 1903 the nearest shopping was in Miami and West Palm Beach. The closest doctor was in Delray Beach.

The population in Hillsborough numbered fewer than 300 around 1900. The Hillsboro River was so clear that it was used by some for drinking water. On February 12, 1901, an act was approved by the U.S. Senate to build a lighthouse at or near Hillsboro Point, Florida. (See Chapter 3, "The Hillsboro Lighthouse.")

By the turn of the century Florida seemed to be the last frontier. Population and per capita wealth were increasing rapidly. Developments quickly attracted buyers. Land was sold and sold again. Profits reached unrealistic plateaus.

The deer population had not changed with the times in Hillsborough, and their presence caused tremendous damage to manmade constructions. The only concession the townspeople were willing to give, however, was a name change. Hillsborough became Deerfield.

In 1909 a school was established in Deerfield. At about the same time another structure was built just south of the Hillsboro River. The building was used by farmers to store their produce; later it served fishermen as a fish-packing house. The building's last use was as the River View Restaurant, which recently closed. In its heyday, Chicago gangsters, including Al Capone, patronized the establishment.

In 1910 the pineapple industry in South Florida collapsed when the business moved to Cuba, where there was better land and cheaper labor. Farmers here were plagued by constant frosts and high freight rates. Still, the railroad remained the best means of shipping produce.

The greatest change in Florida began in the following decade. The government would build or purchase a school and hire a teacher if there were nine children living in an area. In 1911 Hillsboro Inlet qualified, and it got its first school--housed in one of three storage houses already standing at the Hillsboro Inlet Lighthouse Station. Miss Emma Hoff, from Indiana, became the first teacher. The desks were built by one of the lighthouse keepers. Mary Knight, whose father, Captain Thomas Knight, was in charge of the Hillsboro Lighthouse, and John King, who lived on an island across from the light, were among the students.

In 1914 Florida Governor Gilchrist's project of the construction of the Hillsboro Canal was complete. It linked Lake Okeechobee to Deerfield and the Coastal Canal. That same year a telephone line connected Deerfield with Delray Beach. A "toll station" telephone had been installed around 1910 between Deerfield and Pompano Beach.

In 1917 Pompano built a wooden bridge across the intracoastal. The bridge was a swing-type to permit boats to pass. To operate it the bridge tender had to walk in a circle with a big key, turning the gears to swing the bridge open and closed. The road east of the bridge was a sandy, rutted trail that only went a quarter mile or so. The white sandy beach attracted tourists and local residents.

Pompano had been a bit slower than Hillsborough/Hillsboro in getting a post office. The postal record in the National Archives shows that the Pompano Beach Post Office was established as West Pompano in Dade County on April 30, 1900, with Zollie Cavender appointed as the first postmaster. County lines had been redrawn by January 11, 1912, when the post office name was changed to Pompano and the county was Palm Beach.

Part of the "sights" for tourists in the area were the Seminole Indians who frequented the Dixie Highway bridge in Deerfield. They hunted frogs and alligators along the canal and traded with the townspeople.

Even with the relentless progress of development, the people retained their community traditions. Picnics were cherished. Every Wednesday during the summers, the stores would close at noon and people would row across the intracoastal to congregate on the beach.

Dania was the first community in the vicinity to incorporate in 1904, followed by Pompano in 1908 and Fort Lauderdale in 1911. Broward County was formed in 1915 from portions of Dade and Palm Beach counties and named after former Florida Governor Napoleon Bonaparte Broward. Governor Broward had opened the drainage of the Everglades, which had resulted in much of the county's development.

Dredging which had started between St. Augustine and Daytona in 1883 and reached 300 miles to the Hillsboro Inlet in the 1890s was finished in 1914 when it reached Biscayne Bay. The canal was 340.3 miles long. The private dredging company changed hands several times and went into receivership in 1923. By the time the canal reached Hillsboro, the railroad had become the primary carrier of goods. State funds purchased the canal, and title was transferred to the federal government as part of the Intracoastal Waterway system between 1927 and 1931. The waterway was increased to a 125-foot width and a 10-foot depth between 1940 and 1965.

As canals were completed, land sales became increasingly more common. Travel by automobile was also expanded, in 1915 by the completion of Dixie Highway through the eastern portion of Broward County and in 1917 by the erection of a bridge in Deerfield across the intracoastal.

It seemed almost a slap at progress when an influenza epidemic swept the state in 1918. Nearly 30,000 people contracted the disease, and 464 died. The scourge returned in 1919 to take 64 lives and in 1920 to take 79 more.

The people continued to look forward, however. The Women's Club of Deerfield was founded in 1919. Presided over by Mrs. George Emory Butler Jr., the club's first project was to build a pavilion on the beach. As a result of such foresight and work, areas once regarded as worthless were now seen as important for fishing and recreation.

Prohibition entered the era, and rumrunners came to the Hillsboro Inlet and Canal. Prohibition of the manufacture, sale and use of alcoholic beverages had come to the state in advance of the Eighteenth Amendment and the Volstead Act of 1919. Indeed, most counties of the state were already dry, by local option, and Governor Catts made statewide adoption of prohibition a priority. The state legislature ratified the Eighteenth Amendment, and as prohibition progressed, Florida, despite its many dry counties, became a major conduit for illegal liquor importation.

Gun battles were common as government patrols intercepted boats and aircraft from the Bahamas and from distilleries in Cuba. Florida became, by some accounts, one of the wettest states in the nation. As enforcement problems developed, nowhere did the experiment fail so spectacularly as in the city of Miami. Most local officials turned a blind eye to the illegal activities.

Close to Hillsboro Beach, Cap and Lola Knight--who would establish Cap's Place in 1929--became involved in the business of rumrunning. Cap would pick up whiskey in Bimini and return with it to his home near the inlet. The location was isolated, heavily covered with vegetation, and easily accessible to the ocean. His liquor runs were always successful--perhaps, it is said, because he was aided by his brother, light keeper Thomas Knight, who flashed warnings from the lighthouse when the coast was clear. However, Thomas Knight retired as light keeper in 1920. Cap's success, no doubt, had more to do with his superior skill as a navigator and the fact that he had faster boats than the U.S. Coast Guard.

"Hams" was the name given to the burlap bags in which the contraband whiskey was packaged. Cap tied the hams to buoys with a long rope and sank them in Lake Placid. When a customer ordered a bottle, Cap would row out to a buoy to fill the order.

In 1924 electricity arrived, and the following year Deerfield incorporated. Mayor George Emory Butler Jr. and the city council presided over the area.

The population in Deerfield went from 5,135 in 1920, when most of the population were farmer settlers, to 14,242 in 1925, when numbers increased because of an influx of tourists and newcomers whose interests were more urban. That year, 1925, was referred to as "the year of the tin can tourist epidemic." The town did not have accommodations for all the tourists, so they slept in tents in city-sponsored camps, and their meals came from tin cans.

Herbert Malcolm, one of Hillsboro Beach's great pioneers, arrived in the 1920s to purchase 1,000 feet of oceanfront property just north of the Hillsboro Inlet, building the Lake Placid School. After struggling for two years he opened the county's first luxury resort, the Hillsboro Club. (See Chapter 6, "Herbert Lawrence Malcolm: The Lake Placid School and The Hillsboro Club.")

In Pompano the railroad depot was the clearing house for news and information. Six blasts from the train meant bad weather was coming. People were crossing the intracoastal to picnic, not to buy land, for crops would not grow there. Developing much of Pompano's real estate were the Blount Brothers, very prosperous farmers who later donated 23 acres on which they established the State Farmers' Market, the worlds's largest. By 1920, population in Pompano had reached 636.

Leisure life in Pompano also changed. In 1926 the Pompano Race Track and the oceanfront Pompano Beach Bathing Pavilion and Dance Casino were completed. The pavilion featured 100 dressing rooms and shower baths, a first floor dance hall and a second floor orchestra pavilion overlooking the beach. The race track was a mile long and had a grandstand large enough for 6,800 people.

The great land rush of the 1920s reached Florida's Gold Coast, a 70-mile stretch of coastline between Palm Beach and Miami, with dizzying flair. The land boom was the result of many factors, among them national prosperity, transportation and technological development, consumerism, new leisure activities and a fascination with financial speculation. Florida accelerated its already-begun road building program and prohibited inheritance and income taxes. The state experienced a modern day Gold Rush, with its accounts of overnight, instant wealth in real estate.

By the mid 1920s the price of two lots jumped in one year from $6,000 to $150,000. Land was sold and resold. An estimated 6,000 licensed real estate operators stalked the streets of Fort Lauderdale, and thousands worked without licenses. By 1926 the boom had ended, but the area's permanent population had increased significantly.

In June 1925 the Federal Bureau of Internal Revenue agents began examining the profits of South Florida real estate agents. Later the bureau ruled that the entire amount of the selling price for real estate had to be reported as income. Speculators who had been fortunate enough to receive 20 or 25% of sale prices in cash, making them paper millionaires, began to slow down in their real estate activities.

The Florida East Coast Railway, unable to handle the exploding demand for the shipment of building supplies, in 1925 declared an embargo on such shipments to southeast Florida, later extending the sanction to include smaller commodities. The shortage of building supplies assured a collapse of speculative prices. Laborers were discouraged, housing shortages led to rent profiteering, and complaints over prices extended to many goods and services. Because of numerous allegations of fraudulent land promotions, the National Better Business Bureau investigated and found some charges to be valid. The bad publicity and financial decline in the stock market led to investor hesitation and the default of payments by many speculators.

The year 1926 also brought tragedy. A September hurricane destroyed the beach and devastated the region. The Seaboard Air Line Railroad reached the area the following year, in 1927.

In 1928 another disastrous storm struck, destroying property in the area and plunging South Florida deeper into economic depression. After financial security was lost in 1929, the 1930s were a time of struggle.

Following the depression, the center of agriculture in North Broward moved south to Pompano; consequently the train seldom stopped in Deerfield. In 1939 Hillsboro Beach came into being, and Deerfield changed its name to Deerfield Beach in an attempt to make it more attractive to tourists. Its population on the increase, the major sources of employment were the construction of William L. Kester's cottages, the maintenance of Federal Highway U.S. 1, and employment at the Boca Raton Hotel and Club. People were drawn together by a common sense of poverty. Officials worked without pay, and real estate values dropped so low that many people abandoned their homes and properties.

With World War II came an ocean war, and Hillsboro Beach had a front row seat. Many rumors circulated, and because of wartime secrecy much was not documented. Among the rumors, on May 4, 1942, was the claim that the U.S. Navy had apprehended a Nazi submarine on the surface and sank it in 380 feet of water off Dania Pier. The German survivors were said to have been brought ashore in Fort Lauderdale and treated at Broward General Hospital.

German submarines patrolled the shipping lanes offshore and torpedoed ships within a few miles of the beach. Due to government censors, little about the action appeared in the newspapers. After a U.S. Navy boat hit an obstruction in 1943 or '44, a new policy went into effect: navy personnel had orders to blow up shallow water wrecks which were hazardous to navigation. The successful execution of that policy is one reason why there are few identifiable 20th century shipwrecks off our coasts.

During the war, population increased in northern Broward County when the U.S. Army Airfield was established in Boca Raton, just north of Deerfield Beach. Even though Deerfield Beach was still experiencing the effects of the Depression, its citizens were responsive to the war effort. A submarine watch tower was erected on the beach and manned by volunteer citizens around the clock. Many ships had been sunk along the coast. Lt. Jack Nelson, commander of Port Everglades during World War II, was in charge of anti-submarine operations.

A present day Hillsboro Beach citizen, Dean Lindstrom, arrived in 1942 as First Lieutenant and rented rooms in Hillsboro Beach for $65.00 a month. Obtaining housing had become difficult, and U.S. Army officers were billeted at the Boca Raton Club. Dean learned radar at the airfield, where Florida Atlantic University is now located. He tells how all homes during the war had to have lights out at night; the practice was called "black shutters." The intracoastal was also darkened, and cars had to have lights out or blackened with tape so that only slits of light showed through.

Gradually tourism replaced farming, and Deerfield Beach continued--and continues--to prosper. The old way of life is still remembered, however, and homage is paid to those early pioneer farmers in the town's annual Cracker Day--now called Founder's Day--celebration. On this ground where rugged settlers met daily challenges with grit and perseverance, we honor the past and await the future, eager to be part of history as it unfolds.

1
Shipwrecks and Treasure

Scattered references to shipwrecks along the reefs and beaches of Broward County are seldom accompanied by accurate locations. From written accounts as well salvaged ships, we know that the earliest wrecks were usually Spanish. By the late 16th century, however, non-Spanish ships became more numerous, sailing past Florida's coast in order to return to Europe. Portuguese, Dutch and English ships appeared first, then later, French and British pirates and privateers. American colonial ships became common in the 18th century. When returning to Europe, many ships passed within a few miles of Broward County, using the New Bahama Channel.

Spanish navigators, believing it was more important to sight a dangerous reef than to not know its position, steered straight for the dangerous areas. Using this method, ships that left Havana for Spain--laden with gold pillaged from Peru and Mexico--would head directly for the Florida Keys. A northerly course was taken after the Keys were sighted, with the ships staying within sight of the Florida coast until the sighting of Cape Canaveral. After that, Bermuda was the next sighting point.

For protection against pirates, the treasure ships sailed in convoys of fifteen or more galleons, accompanied by Spanish men-of-war. But the convoys could not protect against storms.

Eight ships were recorded shipwrecked as early as the 1500s by Don d'Escalente Fontaneda, who had been shipwrecked and lived with the Tequesta Indians until his rescue near Cape Canaveral. Many other shipwrecks followed over the coming centuries, with a number of the ships being beached after their battering by vicious storms.

One of the most famous fleet disasters occurred in 1715. Eleven slow, heavy Spanish galleons and a French ship set sail at sunrise on July 24 from Havana. Barometers began to fall on Monday, July 29, and although the seas were smooth, the swells were long and menacing to the eyes of the older sailors. By mid-afternoon the ships' lanterns had to be lighted.

By late Tuesday the winds had increased and blown the seas to great heights. The log on the one ship that survived showed that they had not yet sighted Canaveral when the storm and fleet met head on.

At two o'clock Wednesday morning, winds were recorded at 100 miles per hour, and the great Spanish galleons crashed on the shoals of Florida's aptly named Gold Coast. Fourteen million dollars in jewels and metal went down with the ships. Only the French ship escaped. Its captain, disobeying orders, had sailed more to the northeast, directly into the storm. It has been reported that about 1500 people reached shore, but many of those died of exposure, thirst and hunger before help could reach them from Havana and St. Augustine.

In salvage efforts that lasted about four years, the Spaniards recovered almost half their treasure. Through the years others have plundered the remains of that disaster, but there is still treasure remaining in the sand.

A wreck located directly off the present-day Barefoot Mailman Hotel in Hillsboro Beach is thought to have run aground during the 18th century. Worked extensively in the 1950s by Dwight Miller, the salvage effort yielded the ship's hull structure, a cannon ball clump, several cannons and a number of silver coins. The larger salvaged items were displayed at Ancient America, a museum that was located on Federal Highway. Whatever bounty might have remained with the ship continues to be a mystery, for the shifting sand of the ocean has buried the ship and any treasure it might contain.

Another Spanish ship, the *Gil Blas*, was driven aground by a hurricane in September 1835. The ship was bound for Spain from Havana with a cargo of sugar and cigars; it was beached near the Hillsboro Inlet. One family, that of William Cooley, was massacred at New River while Cooley and other New River settlers were salvaging the wreck, which they later destroyed to prevent the Indians from removing the six tons of lead that remained. In 1977 the Marine Archeology Advisory Council investigated a hull, copper tank and long keel, north of Hillsboro, believing that it was the remains of the *Gil Blas*.

In 1871 a schooner carrying a large load of mahogany was wrecked near the Hillsboro Inlet. Six years later the British barkentine *Georgie* ran into a bad storm and suffered total loss. The site of the wreck is thought to be where the Hillsboro Beach hotel The Barefoot Mailman stands today.

On April 19, 1913, the schooner *Alice Holbrook*, carrying a cargo of railroad ties, ran aground on a reef eight miles north/northeast of Fort Lauderdale Station #4 (near where the Bahia Mar Hotel stands today). The captain stayed at the Hillsboro Lighthouse for several weeks, hoping to salvage his ship, but it was destroyed in a second storm. Thomas Knight was the lighthouse keeper at that time.

The captain of the *Alice Holbrook* might have wished for some help when she first went aground. However, in the early 20th century, the beach area here was still sparsely inhabited; shipwrecked passengers and crew held little hope of rescue from friendly settlers or passersby.

To fill that need--and to make themselves a bit richer--men called "wreckers" prowled the beach looking for ships in trouble. These burly, uncouth, yet skilled, salvagers risked their own lives to rescue the people and cargoes of endangered vessels. Who could deny such a "hero" whatever reward he requested? The *Alice Holbrook*'s captain--or any other--who waited in vain to salvage his cargo would have welcomed a few stalwart wreckers, no matter what the cost of their services.

Beached booty was not always claimed by captains, crews, passengers or wreckers. For years, shipwrecks provided supplies to settlers living on the coast of Florida. Such items as lumber, guns, sugar, coal, silver, railroad ties and rum were to be found on the beach, simply for the taking. Going to the beach to look for supplies became as popular a pastime as going to the beach to look for shells today.

The best known shipwreck in Hillsboro Beach has been the one which was for many years a local landmark. It was located partly in the restaurant which also pays tribute to a local legend with its name, The Barefoot Mailman. In January 1976, an article by Sharon Hodges appeared in the *Deerfield Beach Observer* describing this restaurant and bar, named the *Mary Celeste*:

> *The sea was calm the weather fine.*
>
> *The sails of the 103-foot brigantine were set as she sailed with the wind.*
>
> *But the ship circled helplessly. So erratic was her course in the waters of the mid-western Atlantic on the afternoon of December 4, 1892, that a party*

from another brigantine decided to board her. Both ships had taken on cargo a month earlier in New York.

They found the table set and a hearty meal for the captain, his wife and daughter and their eight-member crew simmering in the galley.

Toys were scattered on the captain's bed where a child had been playing.

The cargo, 1700 barrels of alcohol valued at $42,000 was secure in the ship's hold.

But the brigantine Mary Celeste *was empty--even the cat was gone.*

Today, over 103 years later, her hull dominates the dining room of The Barefoot Mailman Hotel in Hillsboro Beach.

How did the *Mary Celeste* find her way to a hotel on A1A from the notorious waters of the Devil's Triangle, that mysterious area of the western Atlantic where countless ships and aircraft and their crews have disappeared?

The question sounds almost too incongruous to ask. One expects a lengthy discussion of salvaging, selling and dealing along with a few words about that all-American business savvy for the unusual.

Instead, the mystery that already surrounds the Mary Celeste is only compound[ed]. "We just don't know," replies Gloria Martin, who with her husband John purchased The Barefoot Mailman Hotel from the Palm-Aire Corporation in May 1974.

Their son Don, who manages the hotel, sheds a little light on the puzzle. "I understand it was towed to a Florida port, probably Miami, and then sailed again until it was dry-docked around 1912. One of our customers told me the story here in the dining room one night," he explains. "I believe it (the hull) was finally sold a little after the war."

But how the hull of the *Mary Celeste* eventually became a part of the hotel dining room they do not know.

Unlike their predecessors, the Martin family along with their restaurant manager Ozzie Ruben, formerly of La Corita in Fort Lauderdale, have made the mystery of the *Mary Celeste* their theme along with the legend of their hotel's namesake, of course the postmen [who used to walk along the beach]. . . .

Inside [the restaurant] the variety of gourmet selections named by Ruben and prepared by Chef Brian Condron, formerly of Cafe de Paris in Fort Lauderdale, describes the area itself--Barefoot Mailman Chowder, Hillsboro Salad, Flaming Steak Hillsboro, Sirloin Palm Beach, Lighthouse Devil's Coffee, to name just a few.

. . . Also authentic is the rope and rigging throughout the dining room. "Captain Bill Cox of the *Gallant Lady* did all the work for us," Ruben adds.

. . . Both agree that recent interest in the Devil's Triangle has helped them. "So many books and articles have been written about it lately," remarks Mr. Martin.

"And every one of them mentions the *Mary Celeste*," adds Ruben.

Indeed, Lawrence David Kirsche, author of *The Bermuda Triangle--Solved*, concedes, "No account of sea mysteries would be complete if it did not include the *Mary Celeste*."

As his title suggests, Kirsche provides a logical though often circumstantial explanation for every mysterious disappearance on the Triangle. But even here perhaps the most skeptical of all researchers into the Devil's Triangle, admits that despite dozens of solutions, simple to bizarre, no one knows what really happened to the *Mary Celeste*.

No one ever will.

* * *

In April 1988, the restaurant--where Charley Brown's now stands--was destroyed by fire. The hull of the *Mary Celeste* and other collector's items were lost.

Today Captain Howard Leventhal, president of Historic Shipwreck Expeditions in Fort Lauderdale, utilizes modern technology, a magnetometer, sidescan sonar, underwater metal detectors and other equipment to explore the ocean floor off Broward County. He chooses to be called an archaeologist rather than a treasure hunter. Having signed a contract with the state Division of Historical Resources, he is authorized to explore an area off Pompano Beach extending about two miles south from the Hillsboro Inlet.

Most treasures found in the area in the 1960s have found their way into private hands. Leventhal, a native of Indiana and salvage operator for nine years, helped treasure hunter Mel Fisher excavate the Spanish fleet that was destroyed in 1715 off Fort Pierce. Bob Sheridan, a Pompano Beach dive charter captain, will coordinate dive operations when the search begins. Leventhal isn't sure how long it will take to find what they are searching for, but he believes there are definitely shipwrecks off the coast.

Numerous wrecks may lie hidden beneath the sea and sand off Broward County's 25-mile coastline or near the Hillsboro Inlet, and with proper archaeological investigation and research, they may yield the answers to many questions and uncover many new puzzles regarding the region's past.

2

The Barefoot Mailman

The barefoot mail route was so named because the carriers walked barefoot on the hard sand at the water's edge. These men have come to be known collectively as the Barefoot Mailman. The carriers' route was approximately 68 miles long, 28 miles by small boat and 40 on foot along the beach.

There was a special gait used by the men who walked the route to keep their legs from hurting. Once a barefoot mailman learned to step a little quicker with the foot which was on the higher sand, he was considered an accomplished beach "walkist."

Ordinarily mail pouches were made of cowhide, but for the beach they were made of lightweight canvas, about 15 inches wide and 30 inches long. They could be rolled up or carried over the shoulder. Each man carried a knapsack for personal belongings and food, such as fish he caught or turtle eggs and oysters he gathered along the way. Once in awhile, however, if one had been especially successful in fishing for his supper, an extra fish would find its way into the mail bag if there was no room in the knapsack.

Each Monday the mailman would leave Palm Beach, row a boat to the foot of Lake Worth, then walk five miles to the Orange Grove House of Refuge (established for shipwrecked sailors) in Delray Beach, where he would spend the night. The next day he walked 25 miles, crossed the Hillsboro Inlet by row boat, then traveled on to the New River House of Refuge in Fort Lauderdale, where he spent the night. On the following day he would row a boat four miles, down to the south side of the New River Inlet, take to the beach again for ten miles of beach walking, thus reaching Baker's Haulover at the head of Biscayne Bay. Twelve miles down the bay, a rowboat would take him to the post office at Miami. He would spend the night in Miami, leave the next morning and return to Palm Beach by Saturday afternoon.

One might wonder how the mailman could be sure of having a row boat each time he had to traverse a waterway. He didn't drag one along behind him, you can be sure. At each water crossing, a boat was always waiting where the carrier had left it. At that time there was a strict, unwritten code against taking someone's boat and leaving it on the opposite shore. In South Florida such an act was comparable to stealing a horse in the old west.

The week-long route was a great improvement over the mail route available before 1885. Prior to that year, a letter from Palm Beach to Miami began its trip at the lighthouse community of Jupiter, 22 miles north, then by an Indian River steamboat to the rail head at Titusville. By train it continued to New York's port and from there by steamer to Havana. From Cuba, a trading schooner took the letter to Miami. It took a voyage of 3,000 miles and a period of six weeks to two months for a letter to arrive in Miami. When the United States Post Office decided to improve its Florida service in 1885 by establishing the barefoot route, it was a welcome decision.

When the job was put out to bid, one of the men interested in the route was Lake Worth resident Edward Ruthven Bradley, a retired Chicago newsman who later became Dade County School Superintendent. Bradley won the contract, which called for one round trip per week for the salary of $600 per year. The job was very demanding, but he and his eldest son, Louie, took turns carrying the mail for about two years.

The Bradleys gave up the contract in early 1887, and the Matthaus brothers, Frederick and Otto, took over. Both brothers walked the route, but they also hired other men to carry mail along the beach route. One of these was James E. "Ed" Hamilton, who had come to Hypoluxo Island from Trigg County, Kentucky. Thinking the task of walking the beach would be more enjoyable than farming tomatoes, he was eager to start.

Stormy weather came regularly near the end of September and early October in 1887, so that all the low lands were under water. On October 10, Ed arrived in Hypoluxo with the mail pouch from Palm Beach, having rowed 10 miles in his small skiff. Although he mentioned that he was not feeling well, he insisted on continuing his trip. Due back on Saturday noon, he did not return.

Suspicion focused on a stranger noticed by Charles Coman, the keeper at the Fort Lauderdale Station (New River House of Refuge). Coman had heard the stranger coming from the beach, having arrived from the north. When the station keeper had asked the stranger how he crossed the inlet, the reply was that a party of hunters at the inlet brought him across in their portable boat. Was the stranger lying? Could he have used Hamilton's boat and left it on the opposite side?

Two of Hamilton's friends, Louie Bradley and Charles Pierce, came down by boat, a 21-mile trip, to follow the route and search for the missing mailman. When they arrived at Hillsboro Inlet, the boat Hamilton would have used had disappeared. His mail pouch, trousers and shirt were hanging on the limb of a tree. They also found a spoon and a bottle of pain killer, and near the edge of the water were Hamilton's underclothes, showing that he had left them to swim the inlet. The indication was very plain: he had seen his boat on the other side of the inlet and had plunged into the water to retrieve it.

To Hamilton's friends, the possibility of his drowning was out of the question, for he was an excellent swimmer and the current at this spot was not very strong. There were sharks here at this time of year, but there was no sign of any when the search was taking place. There were, however, numerous alligator tracks. The place was swarming with them. Even an excellent swimmer might not have escaped them.

Years later a cruising party, spending a few days in Hillsborough, found part of the jawbone of a man that had a gold-filled tooth sticking in it. No one, however, could remember if Hamilton had any gold-filled teeth.

The stranger whom Coman had suspected of foul play was later charged with tampering with government property (Hamilton's row boat) and was tried in Federal Court in Jacksonville. He was acquitted, and his name was never entered in the court records.

The barefoot route was continued until 1892 when a rock road was completed from Jupiter to Miami. The Bay Biscayne Stage Line took over the mail contract at that time. Henry John Burkhardt, who settled at Hillsboro Inlet in 1891, was the last of the barefoot mailmen.

The names of ten of these historic walkers are still known, but the number was greater than that. At one point, any hardy traveler heading north out of Miami or south out of Jupiter was pressed into service. Other mail carriers who were paid to regularly walk the barefoot route were George Charter, George Sears, Edward C. Pent and Andrew Garnett. Garnett later became Dade County Treasurer, school board member and Hypoluxo Postmaster. The town of Hypoluxo was then in Dade County but is now in Palm Beach County.

Another famous walking mailman--in a different part of Florida--was James Mitchell "Acrefoot" Johnson. Apparently he had rather large feet, and at the age of 24 he received a contract from the government to carry mail from DeSoto County to Fort Meade, a journey of 65 miles, which he covered in a single day. That *feat* is still on the postal records. Acrefoot was also fast. As the story goes, a traveler in a horse and buggy suddenly found Acrefoot walking abreast of his carriage. When he offered the mailman a ride, Acrefoot replied, "No thanks, I'm in sort of a hurry."

Wishing to earn more income, Acrefoot decided to carry passengers in a wooden chair strapped to his back. The postal service ordered him to discontinue the practice, so he resigned from the postal route.

The term Barefoot Mailman was used for the first time in Theodore Pratt's book of that title, published in 1943. The walking carriers have been immortalized in several ways, not only in books by authors other than Pratt, but also in a 1951 movie starring Robert Cummings. The mail carriers' accomplishment is kept alive by annual Boy Scout Barefoot Mailman hikes along the beach.

On the grounds of the Hillsboro Lighthouse on the north side of the inlet is a plaque in memory of the most famous of the carriers:

In Memory of
JAMES E. HAMILTON
United States Mail Carrier
Who Lost His Life Here In Line of Duty

Another local landmark which paid tribute to the Barefoot Mailman was the restaurant in Hillsboro Beach by the same name. Although the restaurant burned down in 1988, a monument on the beach remains. Dedicated to these brave men, it reads:

In Memory of
THE BAREFOOT MAILMEN
WHO TRAVERSED THESE SANDS
FROM PALM BEACH TO MIAMI
IN THE LATE 1880s

* * *

In 1956 a branch of the Pompano Beach Post Office was dedicated to James E. Hamilton. According to Terri Whittier, retail sales associate at the branch office, there was a time when mailmen took a yearly hike on the anniversary of Hamilton's disappearance.

Pompano Beach's Golden Jubilee in 1958 received a national publicity boost one spring morning when 22-year-old Glen Courson left the Hillsboro Lighthouse, rowed across the inlet, had a sack full of mail stamped at an antique post office, and trekked down the beach to Miami along the route followed by his legendary predecessors. Upon his return Courson was met by crowds, cameramen and distinguished officials. Unlike those who went before him, however, he had not had to sleep on the beach or in refuge houses. Instead he slept at Fort Lauderdale's Yankee Clipper Hotel and Bal Harbour's Americana Hotel. It is doubtful that Courson had to fish for his supper.

3

The Hillsboro Lighthouse

For centuries ships traversed the dangerous waters around Hillsboro Inlet without the aid of a lighthouse. In 1855, Hillsboro Point, Florida, was designated as hazardous for the safe navigation of ships, and a request was made for official recognition from the U.S. Government. Because the U.S. Congress was not eager to assume this financial burden, it rejected the petition 17 times before the bill was passed. At last the official act was approved on February 12, 1901, establishing a "first-order light at or near Hillsboro Point . . . at a cost not to exceed $90,000." Three years later, on March 3, 1903, the requisite money was fully appropriated.

Having a light at Hillsboro Inlet was important for two reasons. First, the two existing lights on Florida's southeast coast were far apart, with one in Jupiter and the other at Cape Florida. If a ship coming from the Bahamas happened to miss the Jupiter light, now it would have a second chance at Hillsboro Inlet to set a safe course. Second, this inlet presented a dangerous reef area. Without a light here, south-bound ships had to change course and go further east to stay in safe waters.

The site that was chosen first, south of the inlet, proved to have unsatisfactory ground. A second site, north of the inlet, was deemed adequate, and condemnation proceedings were begun.

The property owners, Elnathan T. Field and Mary W. Osborn, of Middleton, New Jersey, had purchased the land in 1886 from the Trustees of the Internal Improvement Fund at 70 cents an acre. The Federal Government paid them $150 for the three-acre parcel of land.

Bids for the buildings and station were opened on August 1, 1905. The building contract for construction other than the lighthouse was awarded to the G.W. Brown Construction Company of West Palm Beach, "not to exceed $21,500." Grading was begun and three dwellings, an oilhouse, a storehouse, a wharf, outhouses, walks and fences were completed. The main house was for the lightkeeper and his family; the other two houses were for the second and third lightkeepers and their families. The oilhouse was a small building which contained barrels filled with kerosene, which was used as a primary fuel to burn and light the wicks located at the center of the lens. Some records indicate that a barracks building was used to temporarily house rescued and injured mariners that had been driven upon the reef during storms and inclement weather.

The lighthouse structure itself was manufactured by the Russell Wheel and Foundry Company of Detroit in 1905-06. It was numbered, crated and shipped by steamship from Detroit, for a 4,000-mile journey. The J.H. Gardner Construction Company of New Orleans, Louisiana, was awarded the contract for clearing the land, laying the concrete foundation, and re-assembling and erecting the lighthouse.

Eight huge foundations were placed in a 40-foot circle on the underlying rock, and a ninth foundation supported the central column. Ultimately the lighthouse was anchored to the underlying coral reef. The inner column held circular stairs and provided space for the heavy weights which would rotate the lens through a clockwork mechanism. The service room and watch room were at the top, where the lightkeepers serviced the lamps and rewound the clockwork.

The lens for the lighthouse, a second order Fresnel manufactured in 1905, was purchased from Barbier, Benard and Turenne, 82 rue Cursal, Paris, France, in 1905. Invented by the French physicist Augustin Jean Fresnel (1788-1827) in 1822, these lenses were available in seven orders, or levels, of power, with first power being the most powerful. The lens shipped to Hillsboro Point had an intense light; its 370,000-candle power could be seen by a ship's navigator at a distance of 31 miles in ordinary weather. On a clear night it could be seen 35 miles at sea. The cost of the lens was $7,250.

The heavy light assembly rotated on a reservoir of liquid mercury weighing 400 pounds. This bath of mercury almost completely eliminated friction, permitting light assembly revolutions as frequent as every 15 seconds. The mercury was contained in a heavy and stable doughnut-shaped base and was to be filtered every 10 years to remove any accumulated salt. The lens was made up of a series of delicate glass prisms, made of thousands of thin glass sheets. Each prism was made by hand and could fit only into the exact spot for which it was designed.

Finally, in 1907, the station was completed and the light was installed. A description printed at the time described it this way:

> *The structure is an octagonal, pyramidal, iron skeleton tower with central stair cylinder; the lower third of the structure is painted white; the upper two-thirds and the lantern are painted black. There*

are three white one-and-one half story light-keepers dwellings in a row, about 100 feet to the northward of the light tower and a red brick oilhouse about fifty feet to the westward of the tower. There is also a boathouse near the inlet with boatways sixty feet long.

When the facility was fully functional, Major MacQuirth, U.S. Army Corps of Engineers, Head Engineer, Eighth Engineering District, inspected the facility and authorized the lighthouse to be placed into service. The first keeper, Alfred A. Berghell, was appointed March 3, 1907, and given the title Captain of the U.S. Lighthouse Service. Captain Berghell retained the position until 1911.

The light, which worked with a series of weights and gears, flashed white every ten seconds. When the lightkeeper commenced his watch, he would carry kerosene from the storage tanks, climb the 175 steps to the mantle, or lens, room, fill the Lucerne (fuel canister) with kerosene and check the wick. The lightkeeper would light the wick approximately one hour before sunset and secure it one hour after sunrise.

During the early days the rotation of the lens was governed by a weight hanging from a manila line in the cylinder. The line went up through the watch room, which was located directly below the lens room. The weight was connected to the line, which in turn was connected to a steel drum. The drum was connected to the lens by a series of gears. The size of the weight determined how fast or slow the lens rotated. It took about half an hour for the weight to reach the bottom of the cylinder, at which time the lightkeeper, who was in the watch room, would insert a hand crank and wind the weight to the top again, starting the process all over.

The lightkeeper was responsible for trimming the wicks throughout his watch. This is where the term *wickies* originates. The trimming of the wicks ensured the even burn of the wick and the proper consumption of kerosene throughout the watch. The trimming of the wick and the cranking of the weight would continue throughout the evening. The head keeper and his assistants would schedule their own watches, but more often than not the assistant keepers stood the watches. This was considered a rite of passage to being a full-fledged lightkeeper, assigned the responsibility of one's own light.

Lightkeepers were instructed by the Lighthouse Board to wear linen aprons to prevent the possibility of scratching the lens with such wearing apparel as buttons and belt buckles.

After the light at Hillsboro Point became fully operational, unexplained fires began to be reported in the Florida Everglades. It was a mystery until someone tracked down the culprit: the Fresnel lens. Occasionally when the light was turned off in the morning, the assembly would stop at exactly the angle and position to focus the sun's easterly rays through the prisms, westward into the everglades. To prevent this from happening, a landward baffle was installed; it also served to protect residents from the brilliant light during the night.

The U.S. Lighthouse Board had been established in 1852, and it was effective for a time. By 1910, however, the task of managing all of the country's lighthouses had become too large for an administrative board. Congress established the Bureau of Lighthouses within the Commerce Department and under the control of the Secretary of Commerce. Its function was to regulate all aspects of lighthouses in the United States.

Succeeding Berghell, Captain Thomas Knight was the lightkeeper from 1911-1920. Captain Thomas Knight's four children grew up at the Hillsboro station and attended a school provided there for the children of the lightkeepers.

There were no real roads along the beach, and the nearest town was Pompano, a mile from the seashore. It was a day's trip to reach town. The children enjoyed swimming and other activities the inlet provided.

Captain Thomas Knight's first assistant was B.F. Stone; J.B. Isler was his second assistant. Monthly salaries were $125 for the lightkeeper, $115 and $110 for the assistants.

In 1920, when Isler became captain and keeper of the light, the antiquated wick mechanism was replaced by electricity. Four 250-watt incandescent light bulbs made the light considerably stronger. The barrels of kerosene were removed, and an emergency generator was installed. There was still plenty of activity left for the lightkeepers. The keeper and his two assistants did all the work and maintenance except for the annual painting of the exterior. In addition to such mundane matters, one had always to be ready to rescue the occupants of ships in distress.

The lightkeepers had to be ever vigilant. When things went wrong, the result could be instantly tragic. For example, the tiny needle in the burner of the vapor light could be extinguished in a flash, and repair would have to be made immediately. In stormy weather the keeper had to be ready to warn vessels that came too close to the reefs and sandbars. In case of shipwreck, they had to put out to sea in one or more of their three 12- to 20-horsepower gas boats and assist those in need. Over the years at Hillsboro Inlet, 19 hydroplanes were towed in during various rescues.

The steel stairway which led to the top of the lighthouse kept the lightkeeper safe from wind and weather, but in September 1926, Captain Isler's perception was not of safety! His scheduled eight-hour watch turned into one lasting 32 hours. In the lamp room, 136 feet above the base of the tower, Isler kept the light burning and wrote in his journal:

> *The heavy winds and surging sea kept hammering away at the tower until I was almost certain it would topple into the Hillsboro Inlet. The vibration was terrific. I recall seeing the roof of our boathouse sailing across Hillsboro Inlet. A small boat stored under the lighthouse was carried away along with other equipment. I wasn't scared but I didn't like it a darn bit.*

The 1926 hurricane proved to be quite devastating to South Florida, but the lighthouse remained--and remains--intact. Mary Ella Knight Voss, one of Captain Thomas Knight's children who grew up on the station, remembered the hurricane in a newspaper interview some years ago. Although her father was no longer the light keeper at the time, Mary Ella recalls that the '26 'cane washed out 20 feet of sand from under the lighthouse.

That same year Thomas' older brother, Captain Theodore Knight, settled in Lighthouse Point and built a small store in Wahoo Bay, just opposite the lighthouse. Hurricanes convinced him that his location was too vulnerable, and he proceeded to move inland to what is still called Cap's Place. One of Mary Ella's siblings, Captain Burnham G. Knight, started the charter boat business at Hillsboro Inlet.

The Presidential Reorganization Act of 1939 abolished the Bureau of Lighthouses and incorporated its activities into the United States Coast Guard. On July 7, 1939, the bureau personnel moved themselves and their equipment to Coast Guard Headquarters. Personnel in the lighthouse service were given the choice to either remain in civilian status or convert to a military position in the Coast Guard, with no less pay.

There were two significant--though undocumented--events that were rumored to have taken place near the lighthouse during World War II. While on routine beach patrol, a Coast Guard-mounted horse detachment spotted a German U-Boat lurking close to shore in the waters off Hillsboro Inlet. The patrol leader quickly reported by radio the location of the submarine to Coast Guard Base Six, in Fort Lauderdale. Coast Guard cutters, a U.S. Navy destroyer and navy planes were diverted from patrol to intercept and, if necessary, sink the submarine. The sub would not surrender and was consequently bombed. Eventually it sank on the reef near the inlet.

The more spectacular event was the seizure of the German raider *M/S Arauca* and the arrest of its crew. A Coast Guard lookout at the lighthouse observed what appeared to be a freighter. After alerting the Coast Guard, several cutters, a destroyer and navy aircraft headed for the mock freighter. *Arcura* crew members were observed throwing armament overboard. Coast guard and navy personnel boarded the German vessel, recognizing it as a raider. The German crew was transported to Port Everglades, and the ship was seized and taken to Port Everglades as a war prize.

In 1966 the Hillsboro Lighthouse became the third most powerful light in the world. The four 205-watt bulbs were replaced with two 1,000-watt xenon high pressure lamps. The candle-power was increased to 5.5 million-candle power.

The lighthouse became fully automated in 1974. One U.S. Coast Guardsman remained on site to maintain the lighthouse and the grounds. The assistant keepers' houses were renovated and used as guest quarters for senior coast guard officers and other senior military officers.

On March 2, 1979, the Hillsboro Inlet Light Station was nominated to the National Register of Historic Places.

This was a unique situation for Florida, since the buildings--with the exception of the timer and generator building--dated from the original construction of the complex, having survived with only minor alterations.

In 1995 the 400 pounds of mercury were removed and the lighthouse sandblasted and repainted. The buildings are still original, and one person is responsible for the grounds and maintenance. The U.S. Coast Guard, the Florida Marine Patrol and the police forces of Pompano Beach and Lighthouse Point are responsible for rescues from the lighthouse.

According to Larry Jesse USCG, the light is now a temporary one, with a visibility of 11 miles. It is hoped that the light will be replaced with a more modern one. The newly formed Florida Lighthouse Association aims to promote and seek funding for the lighthouses of the state of Florida.

4

Keepers of the Light

1907-1911

Captain Alfred Berghell, U.S. Lighthouse Service

In 1884, having just graduated from the Russian naval academy, Alfred Berghell changed his destiny forever when he won a duel with a young Russian officer. Not content with disarming his opponent, Alfred insulted imperial Russia by slashing the golden eagles from his adversary's uniform. Berghell's flight to avoid exile in Siberia set the 19-year-old on an odyssey that would take him around the world.

The Berghells were a Swedish family that had migrated to Finland while it was under Swedish and Russian rule. Direct descendants of Vikings, they settled in Wasa. Alfred's father, one of the wealthiest men in Finland, had one of the highest official positions that could be held by a Finn. No one was superior to him in office except the governor general, a Russian appointed by the Czar. Berghell Senior was what might be called lieutenant governor of the northern half of Finland. His first wife was of the nobility. All of her children were grown before Alfred was born, on December 6, 1865.

As a youth Alfred was an oarsman for the young man who later became Russia's last emperor. Young Berghell's sole ambition was to be a sailor. At age 14 his parents sent him on a voyage to America with an older sister and her husband. Although he was booked in a first cabin passage, he preferred to work as a seaman and experience the hardships of sea life.

His ambition only strengthened, and his parents allowed him to enter the Russian naval academy in his home town. The student class at that time was quite rebellious against the oppressive Russians, and Alfred's sentiments followed that tendency. Nevertheless, having completed the course and having met all the requirements, he was about to enter the Russian Navy as an officer. It was not to be, for after a graduation ball the fateful duel and the insult to Russia intervened, the result of Berghell's taking issue with a slanderous remark made by another young officer. When the two decided to settle their differences with their swords in a secluded part of the building, Berghell had no thought of how it would change his life.

Staying in Finland or anywhere else in the Russian domain was impossible for young Berghell after the incident. His uncle, a Finnish senator, signed a passport for him and he slipped away. The young man never returned, instead wandering the world on vessels and steamboats. He acquired part interest in an English vessel and spent several years trading pearls in the south seas.

His many voyages took him to every important seaport in the world, and he went around the globe four times, surveying many shipwrecks and following the sea. His peripatetic existence ended at age 30, when a serious illness caused him to lose his hearing. He was forced to abandon the life he loved.

Alfred went to Australia to recuperate and from there sailed to San Francisco. Enroute, Berghell became a hero.

The cargo of hemp caught fire and threatened to destroy the ship when the captain's bullying tactics caused his crew to refuse his orders to go below. Berghell gained the men's confidence and, despite his poor health, led them into the inferno below to fight the fire. He lapsed into unconsciousness several times, but the fire was beaten and the ship arrived safely in San Francisco. To show their gratitude, the ship's passengers rewarded him with a gold watch, which he carried with him for many years.

For a while Berghell traveled from city to city across the United States. In 1907 he became the first lightkeeper at the Hillsboro Lighthouse, serving until 1911. After retiring to Santa Monica, California, he spent his time studying and working in his garden. Captain Alfred A. Berghell passed away February 20, 1930, after a life of political intrigue, revolution, shipwreck and mutiny on the sea.

1911-1920
Captain Thomas Knight, U.S. Lighthouse Service

Born in 1879, Thomas Knight was a third generation lighthouse keeper, succeeding Alfred A. Berghell on August 1, 1911. Thomas' maternal grandfather was Captain Mills Olcott Burnham, a Vermont Yankee, who came to Florida's Duval County in 1837, became sheriff and later went on to the legislature. In 1853 Burnham was named keeper of the Cape Canaveral Lighthouse, a brick tower built six years earlier. Later Thomas Knight's father, J.S. Knight, was a keeper of the same light, a position he held until his death when Thomas was 13, in 1892. Six years later, in 1898, Thomas Knight became assistant lighthouse keeper of the Cape Canaveral light. He rose to the position of lightkeeper at Jupiter Inlet and served there for five and a half years.

When Knight became lightkeeper at Hillsboro, he brought his wife, Fannie Gray, and their four children,

Burnham Gray, Ellis Moore, Richard D. and Mary Ella. Moving into the largest of the three cottages on the station, they soon felt at home there.

Mary Ella recalls that a wonderful breeze kept insects away and supplies cool. Connected by a breezeway, the house and kitchen were elevated on sturdy brick piers. Rainwater collected on the roof was stored in a cistern under the breezeway, on the kitchen side. Later a fireplace was closed and replaced by a kerosene-burning stove.

The families at the station grew some of their own vegetables, and for a while, on the mainland, deer and other game were plentiful. As development proceeded, however, animals retreated further into the wild grasslands. Occasionally a Seminole hunting or fishing party came by boat to the station to trade. In addition, the lightkeepers' wives traded their homemade sea grape jelly for pickles and preserves made by nearby farmers' wives.

Traveling the inland canals, the schooner *Cypress*, from Charleston, South Carolina, and the buoy tender *Water Lily* brought supplies once or twice a year. Shallow draft boats came more often, bringing such supplies as kerosene, mops, paint and first-aid medicine.

World War I brought many changes to life at the lighthouse station. Using one of the storage buildings as barracks, the U.S. Coast Guard Beach Patrol always kept four signalmen stationed there. They communicated by semaphore (flag waving or beamed light). Occasionally a seaplane landed where the bridge is today, and the pilot would taxi up to the beach next to the marine rail and boat house.

1920-1939

Captain J.B. Isler, U.S. Lighthouse Service

J.B. Isler, assistant to Captain Knight, brought his

wife, Mary Louise, and three children, Zora, Irene and Luther B. to the compound. A daughter, Ruth, and a son, George, who were born in their home at the station, have the distinction of being the first-born children of record at the Hillsboro Inlet.

Isler worked through the bootleg era of the '20s and the development of the '30s. He was on duty during the famous hurricane of 1926.

Lightkeepers who followed Berghell, Knight and Isler have been members of the U.S. Coast Guard:

1939-1943 Boatswain Mate First Class B.F. Stone

1943-1951 Boatswain Mate First Class W. Bennett

1951-1954 Boatswain Mate First Class H. Kandore

1954-1955 Boatswain Mate First Class J.S. Childs

1955-1956 Boatswain Mate First Class J. Miller

1956-1957 Boatswain Mate First Class F. Edelkamp

1957-1959 Boatswain Mate First Class F. Tucker

1959-1961 Boatswain Mate First Class J. Evdokimoff

1961-1962 Boatswain Mate First Class D.F. Thurston

1962-1966 Boatswain Mate First Class F. Warren

1966-1968 Boatswain Mate First Class J.D. Lloyd

1968-1969 Boatswain Mate First Class J.T. Rodgers

1969-1972 Boatswain Mate First Class D.H. Steerman

1972-1978 Boatswain Mate First Class D.W. Partridge

1978-1981 Boatswain Mate First Class L.W. Jacobson

1981-1984 Damage Controlman Second Class M.B. Sutton

1984-1986 Damage Controlman First Class J.S. Vosburgh

1986-1989 Chief Quartermaster T.M. Golembeski

1989-1993 Electrician Mate First Class M.D. Helms

1993- Damage Controlman Third Class L. Jesse

5

The River View Club

The Hillsboro Canal, once known as the Potomac River, flows into the Intracoastal Waterway at the back door of the Riverview--originally called the River View Club. Today it still has one of Florida's loveliest views, but the Riverview Restaurant remains shuttered, the wooden building quiet; its years of fine dining are at rest.

William Stewart, founder of the River View Club, began his life in Wheeling, West Virginia; he might have stayed there had it not been for the wanderlust he and his brother, Walter, acquired during World War I. As a youngster, William had sold newspapers at the cigar stand in the lobby of the upscale hotel Sarah McClure in downtown Wheeling. He later became a page in the West Virginia State Senate.

Walter, four years older than William, also learned the art of selling as a newsboy. In addition, he learned first hand the rigors of hard labor, working in his late teens as a hod carrier for a masonry contractor. He later had a boxing career, with William as his business manager.

The brothers joined the U.S. Army together, but they were separated after basic training. Walter, stationed in England, helped build airdromes (hangers); William, in France, manned a railway mounted canon.

Around 1924, perhaps feeling bored in Wheeling, they set out to find their fortune by going to Havana, Cuba. Upon arrival they were taken on as trainees in the casino at the Hotel Nationale. After becoming full-fledged croupiers, they began a campaign to encourage their American friends to come to Cuba. From government friends in Charleston, West Virginia, to acquaintances in the sports world, people started showing up in Havana.

No matter how many came south to visit, however, Walter did not feel thoroughly at home, and his homesickness took him back to Wheeling in 1927. There he entered the restaurant business and married his long-distance sweetheart, Esther Wasemann. Two years later, on Christmas Day, their first child, W. William Stewart, was born.

The child's Uncle William followed his brother home to the states, but he settled in Hollywood, Florida, acquired his own roulette wheel and attracted many fans to the Hollywood Circle Bar. Running roulette became a way of life for William, and he always seemed to be heading for the action, going as far north as Saratoga, New York, and other favored locations.

In 1933-34, William became associated with Cap's Place, in Lighthouse Point. At Cap's, Stewart was involved with running the casino activities until sometime in 1937, when he decided to work on his own.

At that time he became close friends with "Red" Lawrence, who was grounds superintendent at the Boca Raton Hotel and Club. Having many good contacts, Lawrence knew about a frame packing house at the water's edge in Deerfield Beach. The two men decided this building was an excellent location for a casino. The building, owned by a Pompano Beach entrepreneur named William Kester, served the native farmers and fishermen of the area. Lawrence helped Stewart negotiate the purchase of the packing house.

Stewart proceeded to add a kitchen and barroom. Wishing to have all in readiness in time for the 1939 season, he asked his contractor to leave one wall of the barroom unfinished. He had located a beautiful, hand-finished, pegged, mahogany bar from a bankrupt night club in the Palm Beach area, and was having a bit of difficulty finding a truck large enough to haul the large, single piece into the club. Once the delivery was made--through the opening left by the contractor--and the barroom could be finished, a hidden room was constructed behind the bar for the roulette equipment and players. While gambling was not legal, it was condoned by the local politicians, and the room provided privacy and security.

Members of both domestic and international society were drawn from the Boca Raton Hotel and Club and the Hillsboro Club. The guest book included such diverse names as Charles Stradella, chairman of GMAC; Frederick Renschler, founder and CEO of Pratt and Whitney; Gerald Coughlan, world-renowned Olympic track star from Ireland; Bernard Baruch, FDR's confidant and financial advisor, and many others of notable stature.

During World War II when a U.S. Army Air Base was established in Boca Raton, many pilots were housed at the Boca Raton Hotel. The River View became a hangout for them. Stewart had already established a policy of not allowing area residents to gamble at his establishment. He extended the restriction to apply to soldiers. They were far from being rejected, however, for all food and beverages were *gratis* to military personnel and regular patrons.

Organized crime reached Florida at the end of the war, and gambling's slide into oblivion began. U.S. Senator Estes Kefauver denounced gambling in his unsuccessful campaign to win the Democratic nomination for the U.S. presidency. Kefauver and casino gambling faded into obscurity together.

When William Stewart died in 1950 as a result of hypertension and stress, the Riverview, as it had come to be known, was operated by his widow, Mae, until she passed away a year later.

Arthur and Eleanor Brown leased the restaurant until 1962. When their contract expired, the current owner, William Stewart, son of Walter and nephew of the original William, took over catering to patrons, many of them rich and famous. His wife, Betty Jean, oversaw all the office work. When adding a 30-seat dining room at the east end of the property, the new owner made sure it was faithful to the style of the original River View Club. Some of the original gambling paraphernalia still adorned the walls when it closed in 1996.

Today the Riverview remains by the water, dwarfed by condominiums and the Hillsboro Bridge. Bill Stewart would like to see the Riverview on the National Register of Historic Places.

6

Herbert Lawrence Malcolm

The Lake Placid School and The Hillsboro Club

After nearly 75 years, The Hillsboro Club is still referred to as the "best kept secret on the ocean." Occupying one of the choicest pieces of real estate in Broward County where the Atlantic meets the Hillsboro Inlet just north of the lighthouse, the club is concealed by trees and shrubbery. Established in 1925 when Herbert Lawrence Malcolm turned from being headmaster of a boy's school to being a club owner, it has survived the assaults of hurricanes, fire and time.

Born on December 12, 1884, Frahran, Colony of Victoria, County of Bourke, Australia, near Melbourne, Herbert was the fourth son of Richard Lawrence Malcolm, a merchant from Oswego, New York, and Martha Anna Crawford of Beechworth, Victoria.

Herbert came to America to go to school, and he graduated from Yale University in 1907. Following graduation he taught at the Lake Placid, New York, School for Boys, which held spring and fall terms in the Adirondacks and its winter term in South Florida. He moved on to teach at Choate from 1909 to 1914. While teaching at Choate he married Helen Parsons of New Haven, Connecticut.

The years at Choate were interrupted for one year while Malcolm took medical courses--part of his resolve to achieve his life-long ambition to become a medical doctor. Family responsibilities, however, foiled his plans. When his mother needed to be taken to California for treatment for her tuberculosis, Malcolm took her. Everything fell on his shoulders, for his brother had passed away from an injury received from falling on a ship. When Herbert returned home, he discovered that many qualifications had been added to the requirements for obtaining a medical degree, and he saw that he would not be able to pursue the career of his choice while carrying out his family duties. He gave up his dream.

In 1914 Malcolm left Choate and returned to the Lake Placid School as both Assistant Headmaster and Director of Athletics. Established in 1905 by John M. Hopkins, the school's purpose was to provide college preparatory education for the sons of Lake Placid Club members. In 1921 Hopkins was forced to give up his duties at the school because of his ill health, leaving all leadership responsibilities with Malcolm. For a number of years the classes held in New York were housed in various buildings of the Lake Placid Club; until 1922 its winter term classes met in Coconut Grove. From 1922 to '25, winter classes were held in Pompano (Hillsboro). The school's fashionable reputation derived from its being small and limited, as well as from its high tuition and its Florida term.

In 1925, after 20 years of being a private school, it was taken over by the Lake Placid Club Education Foundation. Three years later the school's name was changed to Northwood School. The foundation that took over the school had been established by Melvin Dewey to aid schools in the Lake Placid, New York, area. Dewey, who invented the Dewey Decimal System for libraries, was also the founder of the Lake Placid Club. His son, Dr. Godfrey Dewey, was at one time the President of Emerson College and was once chairman of the Northwood School Board of Trustees; he headed the Olympic Committee in 1932.

Life in Lake Placid was appealing, but the winter term in Florida was fascinating. Life was very rustic, for there was not yet a bridge at the inlet and small boats had to be used to cross it. In 1922, having succeeded Hopkins, Malcolm acquired the land at the Hillsboro Inlet and moved the school from Coconut Grove. The school grounds were part of a parcel that had been sold by the state in 1895 to a private investor for 75 cents an acre. In 1922 Malcolm paid $20 per foot for 653 feet, 8 inches. Adding to his holdings twice more, he paid $50 per foot for 100 feet and, later, $75 per foot for another 200 feet.

Sports and the outdoors were important in both Lake Placid and Florida, but during the term in the south, from January to April, sailing was of the utmost importance. The school's "fleet" included a cruising yacht, a knock-about, seven sailing dories and larks, a launch and a supply of skiffs. For the students and faculty, the privilege of sailing on the school's yacht *Orion*, was a splendid part of the winter session. The 56-foot ketch was rigged with an engine, galley, ice chest, two bathrooms and eight berths. The following is an excerpt from the ship's log:

Sixth Cruise: Friday the 13th (1914)

Destination: Angel Fish Creek and Ragged Keys

The good ship left the school docks at 1:50 with a head wind as usual. We had anticipated a race with the "Pest Ship," commanded by Buzzard, John Henry, and Nichols, but were disappointed as she was stuck on a bank near her mooring. We could see a "blue halo" around her masts.

About 6 A.M., Cocoa decided that the victrola needed playing for a change. As strains of "Bagdad" were rising in the morning air, he heard a loud splashing at the stern of the boat, and shouting "Shark," made a dash for the line, followed by the skeptical and sleepy members of the crew. Sure enough it was a shark, and the united efforts of the crew soon had it up to the side of the boat where Lief beat it over the head with a baseball bat. . . . After pictures had been taken of the seven-foot monster of the deep, we cut off his head for the jaw and consigned the body to his brother sharks. Nothing daunted by this episode, everybody had a dip in the water before breakfast.

* * *

The boys at Hillsboro were considered boys who could carry a tea cup as well as a football. Many were members of American society. Names such as Wood, Beatty, Ehret, Howell, Guest, Rockefeller, Davis, Pinchot and Pirie appeared on the roster.

An accomplished athlete, Malcolm was usually the coach, since he was both headmaster and director of athletics. He was a world traveler and mountain climber, having scaled some of the world's best-known peaks. When in his 50s, he set speed and distance records in the Adirondacks, the White Mountains, and the Clinton Range. At the age of 66 he ascended the 17,800-foot Popocatepetl in Mexico, and at 69 he scaled Switzerland's Matterhorn. At 73 he was clocked at 29 seconds for the 220-yard dash on the Pompano High School running track.

After a two-year struggle with his school and suffering the effects of a financial depression, Malcolm had money problems. With the encouragement of parents of his students, he opened the Hillsboro Club at a place already known as a fisherman's paradise. Guests were offered rooms at $35 per week, American plan.

David Beatty, a former student at the Lake Placid Florida School, had backed Malcolm financially when he moved the school to Hillsboro, but he refused to support the hotel plan--primarily because of an experience he had had while fishing on Lake Worth. There his fishing had been interrupted one day when he saw smoke thickly spreading over Palm Beach. The source of the smoke was the fire which consumed the Breakers Hotel. Witnessing that event soured Beatty on wanting anything to do with a hotel venture.

Nonetheless, Malcolm forged ahead. He built extensions and purchased the lighthouse cottage from the U.S. Coast Guard. The Hillsboro Club officially opened on October 23, 1925, with a winter season lasting from October to February. The restaurant menu presented by the Malcolms, who were their own chefs, offered a "catch of the day," for the local waters provided much variety. The inlet was very shallow, and at low tide one could walk across.

Water was an important consideration. Water pipes under the inlet carried water to the club, but pressure was a problem, and the savvy, experienced guest kept his tub full of water. According to Herbert's nephew Allen Malcolm, who became manager in 1935, water was always a problem. Rumor had it that guests used their gin for bathing when the water pipes broke. An interesting letter from the Pancoast Hotel in Miami Beach was sent to the Board of Water Commissioners, Pompano, on May 28, 1933:

Dear Sirs:

Friends of mine in the north have learned of the fact that fresh water will be supplied to the Hillsboro Club and are anxious to know whether or not the work will be completed this fall. There are three families of them, a party of about twenty, who have gone to southern California for the past two winters. But they will gladly return to the club next season if they can be sure that they will be free from salt water. Mr. Malcolm has treated them royally in former years. Please let me know about it by early mail and I will do all I can to bring them back to Florida.

Sincerely,
Frank Jennison

Years later, however, there was still evidence of a water problem in a message written to club manager Norman Pancoast:

Feb 14/49

We have no water in the morning
We have no water in the night
No wonder, Mr. Pancoast
Your guests are such a sight,
Give us water & we'll look fine
Will you be my Valentine--

Tiny Campbell

Trouble with the water did not make the club unpopular. In its social news in January, 1927, there were listed in the *Fort Lauderdale Daily News* the names of many famous guests who had stayed there. The club entertained only 60 guests at a time, and there was always a waiting list.

The hurricane of 1926 caused extensive damage to the club and its buildings, but Herbert was among the few Floridians who was fully insured against storm losses.

Malcolm worked nearly non-stop to make his resort the ultimate experience for his guests. This was a prodigious task, for in 1929 Hillsboro Beach was still fairly deserted--a wilderness. Indeed, the club's telephone number was Hillsboro Two. There was a bridge over the intracoastal in Pompano by that time, however. Ruby Alexander was the bridge tender.

In 1933 nephew Allen, having just graduated from Yale, came with his wife to visit the club. Herbert asked him to stay on as a bellhop. Allen did so, and later became the manager, working in that position until 1945. In the early years, one of his summer chores was trucking wood from the sawmill in Deerfield for the steam boilers, for in the winter, weather could become cold enough to cause ice to form on a pail of water. Steel radiators were purchased for the rooms.

Helen Parsons, Herbert's first wife, was a collector of bookplates, and she developed the library which is still enjoyed today. She passed away in 1940. Malcolm's second wife was Patricia Edwards, from Lakeland/San Francisco, California. Pat had gone east to work for a Harvard professor, a paleontologist. When the professor moved his lab to Randolph, New Hampshire, she moved with the job. A well-established mountain club existed in the area, and one day when she was hiking on the mountain she met Malcolm, whom she called Bert. Not only did she become his wife, she also worked for him as his secretary in later years. They had two children, Herbert Lawrence Jr. and Mary, and four grandchildren.

Herbert Senior was not content with one resort. He built the Pink Sands in the Bahamas, where Allen later made his home, and he also bought and remodeled the Waumbeck, in Jefferson, New Hampshire.

The Hillsboro Club had no bar, so many guests saw their visit as a family affair. A weekly gathering called the Hymn Sing, on Sunday evenings, has been carried over from those early times and is still enjoyed today.

Guests who wished to drink could have room parties, with a little help from the bellhops. Those who wanted to drink and gamble could also go across the intracoastal to Cap's Place or to Deerfield to the River View Club.

No one believed that Herbert Malcolm would ever leave the club, but managing three resorts took its toll. He began frequently to express the wish that members would buy him out. In 1959 he agreed to sell the club to Kroetz and Keagy, developers in South Florida. Contracting hepatitis while mountain climbing in Mexico, Malcolm died of cirrhosis at the age of 74 later that year--before the deal had come to fruition. His family, however, honored the agreement.

Florida Hillsboro, Inc., the name given to the new project, underwent many new physical changes. The company built the North House, the Tee House, the Terrace Lounge, the pool, and the pitch and putt course. Because some of the additions did not conform to the original architecture, many members feared losing the resort as they had come to know it.

Percival Brundage, a member who had been Director of the Bureau of the Budget under President Eisenhower, formed a group that eventually sold stock and debentures to members, and they were able to buy back the club. In 1962 they formed the Hillsboro Association, Inc. (a Delaware for-profit corporation).

The association leased the property to the club for a fee but held responsibility for its operation. Two boards existed: the Association Board, which handled all management matters and operation, and the club board, which oversaw internal affairs. The two boards made an offer for all Association stock; most investors accepted the offer, selling it back to the club at the original cost of $100 per share. Finally in October 1984 the club owned all the stock.

Norman Pancoast, who began as assistant manager at the club before becoming the manager, continued to perform in that role after Herbert Malcolm's death. His assistant was Norman Sheffield. In 1962 Kenneth Kenyon became the club's manager. He divided his time between managing the Hillsboro Club and the Waumbeck Resort. The staff continued to split their time between the two resorts as well.

Kenyon stayed until 1967, when Sheffield, his wife, Carol, and their children returned to the club. Sheffield was responsible for having the protecting wall built against the foundation of the club buildings. He remained at the club for 19 years, retiring in 1986. Robert Case was manager for two years, then Sheffield returned as interim manager for a season. Daniel Dodge became manager in March 1989 and is still club manager today.

Coincidentally, the beach manager for the Hillsboro Club today is life guard Connie Case, the daughter of former club manager Robert Case. Connie is a former triathlete and two-time competitor in the Ironman. Her efforts for charity include a 10-mile swim down the Intracoastal Waterway for the benefit of Horses and the Handicapped of South Florida, a week-long kayak trip for the benefit of Alzheimer's Disease patients, and a nine-mile swim in Lake Huron as part of a fund-raiser for the refurbishment of a 300-year-old church in Michigan.

During the tenure of developers Kroetz and Keagy, two world-famous tennis pros, Doris Hart and Lois Felix, were hired. They out-lasted their first employers at the resort, staying 29 years and playing a major role in attracting guests.

The establishment continued to grow; new buildings and other additions eventually expanded it to triple its original size. The original zoning of the property, which designated it for hotel club operations, predates the town.

The Hillsboro Club was patronized by national and international dignitaries and blue-book names. Famous visitors include: John L. Lewis, Katharine Hepburn, Bing Crosby, Grosvenor Allen, Edward J. Stettinius (Secretary of State, 1944-45), Prescott Bush, Stephen Footje, Colonel Charles Speaks, Frederic H. Curtiss, Franklin D. Roosevelt, Winston Churchill, the Countess of Hillsborough (sister of Churchill and resident of Palm Beach), and opera singers Richard Crooks and Gladys Swarthout.

Patricia Malcolm remembers Churchill painting on the beach, and Allen Malcolm recalls how the secret service was everywhere, many of them spending time jogging on the beach and in the area.

Fire roared through the Curtiss House and the Malcolm house in 1979. Both were damaged, but the older building, the Malcolm House, was left without heavy loss. The 20-unit Curtiss House, where the fire originated, was gutted. This was not the first time facilities at the club sustained major damage, although pervious destructive events were weather-related. In 1935 and again in 1947 the club was struck by a hurricane. In 1947, 160-mile per hour winds collapsed the glass-walled dining room and uprooted many trees.

In 1988 the board decided that a number of changes were needed. Although many members fought the new plan--clinging to their belief that the club should be true to its original look--time and sea air had added their damage to that brought by wind and fire. Improvements were imperative. In 1991 Malcolm House was replaced with two new buildings. The new Malcolm House now has a spacious lobby with several sitting areas and 14 new bedrooms. The other new building was named Herschede House for the late Mark Herschede, whose support helped push the renovations. It holds a gift shop, library and 32 bedrooms with balconies. Everything was built in an amazing eight months. In April 1992 the dining room, kitchen and

Hogan's Alley were replaced by Van Dusen House, named after the former Chairman of the Board, Dick Van Dusen. This new building houses a kitchen, dining room and six bedrooms, all with ocean views.

Having recently opened to summer memberships, the club continues to change with the times. There are 10 Har-Tru tennis courts, a nine-hole chip and putt course, a fresh-water pool, a library, a masseuse, an exercise and game room, a beauty salon and a gift shop. The club has also joined an environmental cause, joining with Broward County, Nova University and the Florida Environmental Protection Program to preserve Florida's sea turtles.

"There are several things that I'm most proud of about the club," says Daniel R. Dodge, the club's general manager. "They are the enjoyment that people derive from just being here, and the fact that we've maintained not just the physical setting but also the style that's been successful for such a long time. Most people don't even know we exist. We have such wonderful facilities and are proud to be involved in the community."

Nearly 75 years ago Herbert Lawrence Malcolm started a school and then established a club, which still endures as an exclusive resort. In addition to founding these institutions, he also managed them for 34 years. Moreover, he was a charter member and a president of the Pompano Beach Rotary Club, became one of the founders of the town of Hillsboro Beach, served as one of the three original commissioners, and was both a vice-mayor and mayor of the town. He was a driving force in the development of Hillsboro Beach.

PHOTOGRAPHS

1935 - Hillsboro Beach

1953 - Cap's Place in background, Old Town Hall, Johnson Residence

1949 - Stettenius Residence

Herbert Lawrence Malcolm - 1885-1959

Ernest Wooler - 1888-1969

1950's - Hillsboro Inlet

1940's - Hillsboro Club

WAR MEASURES AT HILLSBORO LIGHTHOUSE

Whether it be peace or war there will be no secret spying around the Hillsboro Lighthouse and no bombs exploded under its foundations if your Uncle Samuel can prevent it. Excursionists going from here to the lighthouse since the breaking of diplomatic relations with Germany have been met by an armed guard and turned back. The regulations allow no one on the government property at Hillsboro lighthouse without a pass. Visitors to the lighthouse now either stop on the west side of the bay or cross over to the south side of the inlet and look at the lighthouse from that safe distance and watch the guards on their beat.

February 28, 1917 - Sentinel article

(ALL COMMUNICATIONS TO BE ADDRESSED TO THE COMPANY)

OFFICES		TELEPHONES	TELEGRAMS
MANCHESTER	COOKE STREET, HULME (REGISTERED OFFICE) TRAFFORD PARK	772 AND 3553, NATIONAL 4031 NATIONAL	[illegible] MANCHESTER SWITCH MANCHESTER
LONDON	20, BUCKLERSBURY, E.C.	5430 BANK	[illegible] LONDON
BIRMINGHAM	9, SHIRLEY ROAD, ACOCKS GREEN	33 ACOCKS GREEN	ROYCES ACOCKS GREEN
GLASGOW	PARTICK HILL ROAD, PARTICK	754, NAT. HILLHEAD; W492, CORPORATION	ROYCES, GLASGOW
BELFAST	43A HIGH STREET	1154 NATIONAL	[illegible] BELFAST

CABLEGRAMS: SWITCH, MANCHESTER, ENGLAND. CODE: A.B.C. 5TH EDITION

WORKS
ELECTRICAL & ENGINEERING, TRAFFORD PARK.
MOTOR CARS, HULME.

ROYCE LIMITED,

COOKE STREET, HULME.
MANCHESTER.

In replying please quote
D. 1/11.

1st Nov. 1905.

Herbert Wooler Esq.,
99, Bishop St., Moss Side,
MANCHESTER.

Dear Sir,

We are much obliged for your kind cheque to hand value £100 (one hundred pounds) in respect of premium of your son Ernest's apprenticeship, and as the indentures are completed and stamped with one small exception, we shall be glad if you will kindly give the writer a call at an early date so that the matter may be entirely completed and the indentures handed over to you.

Thanking you in anticipation of your kind attention,

We are,

Yours faithfully,

D/B

John DeLooze

1905 - Indenture for Ernest Wooler's Apprenticeship
Courtesy of Michael Evans

HILLSBORO EXPERT ON EROSION
. . . he has made beaches his hobby

Ernest Wooler

1949 - Hillsboro Beach

1950 - Amo Angeletti

1952 - Chuck Kanode

1955 - Hillsboro Beach

JOHN ERICKSON
Mayor 1978-1983

KEITH BROOKS
Mayor 1972-1974

VIEWING MODEL OF OPAL TOWERS are Mr. and Mrs. Walter Schreiber, developers of the Hillsboro Beach Condominium, Hillsboro Commissioner David Healy, Deerfield Commissioner Emerson Church and Hillsboro Commissioner, Chris J. Truelson.

Courtesy of the Deerfield Beach Observer,
October 30, 1969

1970 - Herbert Whiting
Courtesy of Jacki O'Hara

1955 - Town Hall under construction
Courtesy of Jacki O'Hara

1950 - The Aiden (South of The Recess)

1950 - The Recess - Courtesy of Jacki O'Hara

Established in 1953, Hillsboro Country Day School is located at the north limits of beautiful Hillsboro Beach. New CBS buildings, cheery classrooms, a large auditorium, modern kitchen and dining room, and administrative offices comprise the physical plant of the school.

Hillsboro Country Day School - Courtesy of Barbara Bittner

1966 - Opening of New bridge at Inlet.
From left to right:
Chief McMullin, Mayor Woods, Mary Campbell,
Commissioner Anne Rode, Town Clerk M. Froedge,
Commissioner C. Truelson, Ken Rode

1960's - The Barefoot Mailman Hotel

1994 - Lt. Bob Jones

1994 - Abandoned Cuban refugee rafts on beach.

1949-50 - Mayor Wooler and Town Marshal Angeletti with first police/fire vehicle

7

Cap's Place

There it sits, on a peninsula, the oldest restaurant in Broward County and accessible only by boat to its customers. They patronize faithfully this landmark north of Pompano Beach, in Lighthouse Point. Because of its seclusion, it is a little difficult to find, but in or out of season, the dining room has been filled with patrons for nearly a century.

Cap's Place opened for business in 1929, originally known as Club Unique. The restaurant was just as popular in the '30s as it is today.

Eugene Theodore "Cap" Knight, born in 1871 in Cape Canaveral, Florida, came from a family of seamen. His grandfather, Captain Mills Olcott Burnham, a Vermont Yankee, transferred in 1837 from the Federal Arsenal in Watervliet, New York, to the Arsenal of Jacksonville, later serving in the Florida State Legislature. Cap's father, J.A. Knight, served as light keeper at Canaveral from the early 1870s until his death in 1892.

Cap ran away from home at the age of 13 and secured a job as a messboy on a lighthouse tender. He worked his way up to mate, later becoming Master of

Morgan Line Steamers, sailing from New Orleans and New York. By the time he retired he had put in 35 years of service.

His younger brother Thomas later became the keeper of the Hillsboro Lighthouse in 1911 and would reportedly signal Cap as he passed via steamship.

A brother younger than Thomas was Burnham Gray Knight, born in Titusville in 1903. He received his beginning education at the school established at the Hillsboro Lighthouse. In 1914 Burnham began as a fishing guide at the Hillsboro Inlet with a row boat and one passenger, later working up to a small inboard skiff which would hold four passengers. In 1915 he took out his first charter boat and, in order to cover the law, took his father with him. By 1930 he had five charter boats, each holding six passengers. Because of gas restrictions during World War II, he had to discontinue his business.

Burnham ventured into commercial fishing and operated a fish and poultry market in Pompano and Deerfield until 1952, when he returned to charter boating from the Lighthouse Yacht Basin in Pompano. He is credited as being the founder of charter fishing.

Burnham's wife, Minnie Mae Dowling, was born in Georgia in 1909. Coming to Florida as a child, she attended the lighthouse school with the Knight children. It was in the lighthouse, in the neighborhood in which she grew up, that Burnham proposed to her. They were married in 1927 and had three children, William Thomas, Shirley Mae and Linda Jane.

Cap married Bertha Lydia Armour, daughter of James Arango Armour, keeper of the Jupiter Lighthouse from 1866 to 1906. They had three children, two sons and a daughter. The marriage ended in divorce prior to 1914. At the age of 43 Cap married Lola Saunders, 23, the school teacher at the Hillsboro Lighthouse.

By 1926 Cap, at 55, had settled at the inlet and built a small store in Wahoo Bay. It was around this time that he met a young man from Pittsburgh, Pennsylvania, Albert Hasis. The 16-year-old Al, like Cap at age 13, had run away from home and was looking for a way to make his fortune. A close relationship developed that was to last throughout their lives.

The hurricanes of 1926 and 1928 that were devastating to all of South Florida were not merciful to Cap, either. With Al's help he moved his business to the present site, a peninsula bordered by the Intracoastal Waterway on the east and Lake Placid on the west. In Miami, for about $100, they purchased an old barge that was said to have been used by Flagler when he constructed the Overseas Railroad to Key West. Beaching their purchase at its final resting place, they proceeded to build what was to become a local landmark. Iron fittings were stripped from the barge; the cabin and other parts that were removed were sold for scrap. Cap and Al purchased Dade County pine from the newly operating Pompano Lumber Company and built an enclosed structure on top of the barge.

The barge raised the structure a few feet above the ground and served as its foundation. Walking on a wooden boardwalk from the intracoastal, patrons proceeded up three steps that were part of a porch surrounding the building. Two intimate and informal dining rooms made up the eastern section, with walls made of wooden boards identical to those on the exterior. The rooms had pine flooring, open rafters and bare light bulbs, a tradition. Screens were never used, although dark cloth was used on the windows during prohibition for privacy. Within a year there was a need for more space, and other wood frame structures were built. One of the dining rooms was called the yellow room. Between this room and the other dining areas is a corridor that allows service from the kitchen in the northwest section of the building. In this corridor are six nooks which held the slot machines when the restaurant had a casino; today they feature shelves that hold glasses. At the north of this hallway is a small storage room that serves as a wine cellar and office.

The bar used today is the same one that was built in 1928. At the north of the barge, it was constructed by Al Hasis of bamboo from the Everglades and polished wood from ships' decks. The top of the bar, made of old ship's decking, dominates the room, which is decorated with beach memorabilia, photos, parts of ships, rope, driftwood, harpoons, shark jaws, rattlesnake skins, and Cap's collections of mugs and coins. Fishnets serve as curtains. The floor and roof are made of Dade County pine, and the ceiling beams and walls are of pecky cypress.

During the casino years the west side of the room contained a wheel of fortune and private dining alcoves with curtains. These alcoves have been boarded up, but the ambiance of the early days remains.

The roaring twenties ended abruptly in Florida. What the hurricanes of 1926 and 1928 started, the depression finished. The real estate boom was over. Tourism flourished, however, boosted by gambling--legal and illegal.

Cap's Place was an immediate success for several reasons. Its being remote and private was a very important element to the regular clientele. Until 1953 the restaurant was accessible only by water from Hillsboro Beach. Cars would park across the intracoastal and flash their lights until the signal was seen by an employee, who then paddled a rowboat across and ferried the customers to Cap's.

The food was the freshest and most unique in the area. Cap began by doing all the cooking himself. Rolling up his sleeves, he would fry fresh pompano, dolphin, kingfish and green turtle steak. He was famous for his chowder and the enduring hearts of palm salad. An original menu from the early '50s offers a full dinner which included shrimp cocktail, heart of palm salad, French fries, hot rolls, butter, sea grape jelly, coffee or tea and choice of fried shrimp, oysters, chicken, kingfish, mackerel, bluefish or snapper. All this for $2.50. Patrons could get broiled lobster tails for $3.00.

In addition to privacy and good food, Cap's offered gambling, which was illegal at the time. Officials turned a blind eye to these activities. At Cap's, private memberships were sold to the "supper club" for 25 cents. Besides slot machines and a wheel of fortune, other games included blackjack, dice games, chemin de fer tables and a roulette wheel.

In the 1930s, gambling interests who controlled the action told Cap to improve the place. The Poinsettia Room was decorated at that time, and red carpeting was laid in the front dining room. The money-counting room, located at the south end of this room, had a private exit to the east. To keep the casino open, many people were necessarily involved, including local officials and the syndicate. Meyer Lansky reportedly made a weekly trip to Cap's to collect his share of the gambling income, about 10 or 12 percent.

In 1940 Cap taught Sylvester Love, who had begun as a dishwasher, to prepare the meals Cap's way, special for each guest. Chef Sylvester became as much a part of the restaurant as the surroundings. Guests enjoyed their meals in the yellow dining room, cooked by Sylvester and served by Cap, in his bib overalls and denim shirt.

Many famous guests found their way to Cap's. Across the intracoastal were the Hillsboro Club and some homes owned by notables such a Secretary of State Edward R. Stettinius. Alcohol was not served at the club, and Cap's provided a great outlet for the guests who were staying at the resort. Some of the celebrities who dined, and perhaps gambled, at Cap's Place were Prime Minister Winston Churchill, President Franklin D. Roosevelt, General George Marshall, Lord Beaverbrook and Admiral William "Bull" Halsey. Other well known figures from the arts, sports, movies and the social scene included Joe DiMaggio, Susan Hayward, Casey Stengel, Jack Dempsey, James Montgomery Flagg, Kate Smith, Myrna Loy, George Jessel, George Harrison, the Vanderbilts and Al Capone.

In 1945, on vacation from Minneapolis, came a young woman named Patricia McBride, who met and fell in love with Al Hasis. Soon they were married, and a cottage built by William Kester, a wealthy real estate developer, became their home. Both Pat and Al worked at Cap's, and it became their life's involvement.

Cap and Lola had built a house on stilts over the water. Their home for more than 30 years, it later became a boathouse.

In 1951 a congressional investigation of illegal activities in Florida, started by Senator Estes Kefauver, put pressure on Cap with regard to gambling. This ended the weekly visits from mobster Meyer Lansky and his men.

During the early 1950s the city of Lighthouse Point was developed by R.E. Bateman. William Kester, who originally owned the land, sold it in 1951. In 1953 the city platt was officially labeled Cap Knight Bayou. In 1956 the 107 residents voted to incorporate, and it became a city in 1957, 50 years after the founding of the Hillsboro lighthouse.

In 1954 several local businessmen offered to buy and transform the island into the area's first yacht club. The project was to be called the Hillsboro Yacht Club. According to a *Miami Herald* article, Cap was to be named "honorary commodore" and operate his restaurant until 1955. The project was scrapped when the developers could not agree among themselves.

Always the daring entrepreneur, Cap occasionally was confronted by the law. In 1962 he was arrested and charged with possession of illegal turtle eggs. Cap had always made his pancakes with turtle eggs, which he bought from poachers. Amo Angeletti, the first town marshal of Hillsboro Beach, recalls that Cap usually kept several thousand turtle eggs frozen at one time. Fred Cabot was the conservation agent who caught up with Cap, who had been serving the eggs for more than 30 years. Cap was released on bond, and he promised not to buy them again.

Amo Angeletti recalls Cap as a tall, powerful man who was very fond of bib overalls and was always barefoot. He loved to sit by the water and shoot alligators.

In 1964, after living a very adventurous life for 93 years, Cap died. He is buried in the Pompano Beach Cemetery.

Another interesting side of Cap was his refusal to pay income taxes. After his death three appraisals made on the property showed it to be worth $97,600. The government put liens on the property totaling more than $47,000, and when the liens went unpaid until 1968, Cap's was closed. Pat Hasis, Al's wife, agreed to pay the liens and debts to get control of the property. She also agreed to provide housing and care for Lola Knight, Cap's widow, as long as she lived. Lola later retired and moved to Palatka, but until her death in 1989, she maintained an interest in the restaurant.

Cap has been described variously as pioneer, legend and outstanding character. He played a prodigious role in South Florida's history, along with his partners, friends and employees Al and Pat Hasis, Sylvester Love and Lola. Cap was truly a legend of his time.

Today Cap's Place is owned and operated by the oldest Hasis son, Tom, a successful attorney and Lighthouse Point City Commissioner. His sister, Talle, and brother,

Ted, also work to maintain the quality of dining that for so many years has attracted locals and, today, tourists.

A motorboat has replaced the rowboat, and patrons no longer flash their lights from across the intracoastal. The menu is basically the same as it was years ago--without the turtle eggs.

On August 10, 1990, Cap's Place was officially listed on the National Register of Historic Places. It is the oldest standing structure in Lighthouse Point and the only historic site. Architecturally the buildings are referred to as vernacular architecture, in that the builder uses his experience and available materials to create a useful and practical building. It is, in plain language, ordinary architecture that follows no academic style.

A landmark comparable to none other in South Florida, it has withstood prohibition, mobsters, depression, wars, ravages of nature, and many joyful and peaceful times for nearly a century. The area has been greatly developed since that barge was brought ashore, but the ambiance created so long ago will remain intact into the 21st century.

8

The Town Charter

In 1939 Charles Lindford, a Fort Lauderdale accountant who worked for Herbert Malcolm, was engaged to write the town charter. The bill, which he helped create with Malcolm, was filed on June 12, 1939, with the Office of the Secretary of State.

SENATE BILL NO. 1107

An Act To Establish a Municipality in Broward County, Florida, to be Known as the Town of Hillsboro Beach: To Define Its Territorial Boundaries: To Provide for Its Government and to Describe Its Jurisdiction and Powers.

ARTICLE I
CORPORATE NAME

There is hereby created in Broward County, Florida, an incorporated town which shall be known as the "Town of Hillsboro Beach."

ARTICLE II
TERRITORIAL BOUNDARIES

The boundaries of such town are hereby established and fixed to be as follows:

Begin at the intersection of the North line of Section Township 48 South, Range 43 East, with the center line of the right of way of the Intracoastal Waterway (Florida East Coast Canal); thence Southerly along said center line through said Section 8 and Sections 17 and 20, said Township and Range, to a point in a line passing through the center of the draw of the highway bridge across the Hillsboro River at right angles to the center line of the roadway of said bridge; thence Southeasterly along said line through the center of the draw of said bridge to a point in a line parallel to and 553.8 feet South of, measured at right angles to the North line of said Section 29; thence Easterly along said parallel line to the waters of the Atlantic Ocean; thence Northerly along the waters of the Atlantic Ocean to the point of beginning.

ARTICLE III
GOVERNMENT

Section 1. The government of the said municipality shall be vested in a governing body or commission composed of three members, which shall be known as "Town Commission of the Town of Hillsboro Beach."

Section 2. ALBERT J. MARKLAND, HERBERT L. MALCOLM AND J. ALLEN MALCOLM are hereby appointed as and to be the members of the Town commission of the Town of Hillsboro Beach and shall constitute the first Commission thereof and shall serve as such until their respective successors shall be elected and duly qualified.

LAW OFFICES
McCUNE, HIAASEN, FLEMING & KELLEY
BROWARD NATIONAL BANK BUILDING
FORT LAUDERDALE, FLORIDA

TO Town of Hillsboro Beach
Pompano, Florida

November 18, 1947

[Le]gal Services as follows:

Expenditures made in connection with
Charter for the Town of Hillsboro Beach;

Prorated amount of expenses to Tallahassee during the Legislature	$50.00
Publication of notice of bill being introduced into Legislature	2.00
Telephone calls	1.06
	$53.06

Received payment 11/18/47
McCune, Hiaasen, Fleming & Kelley

By Judy Mercer

WJK:

Thank you.

1947 - Charter expenditures

First Decade: The '40s

And so began the Town of Hillsboro Beach, with a bank deposit of $100, half being a donation by Malcolm and the other half a donation by Markland, deposited in the Farmers Bank of Pompano Beach.

The issues at that time, from notes taken at the first meeting of the Commissioners, were listed as follows:

1. Tax roll same value as state and county
2. Ordinance re fire protection from Pompano
3. Money needed for attorney fees, record books, etc.
4. Franchise to Tel. Co. and Fla Power and Light
5. Franchise to Pompano re water supply

6. Make Farmers Bank of Pompano depository for funds.

7. Books needed--Town Clerk, Treasurer Tax roll supplies by Kelly

Ordinance re turtle turning

Arrangement with Sheriff for deputy authority

Ordinance forbidding signs advertising particular property

Ordinance requiring filing of plans for all building in town, but no fee

Ordinance meeting of Council every 6 months--First

Monday in May and November at 2 PM at Hillsboro Club

Deposit $50.00 each from HL & Markland and $100 each from Mitchell & Phipps i.e. Bessemer Properties to be deposited.

Signs at N & S end of town

Adopt state laws as laws of town

Bird Sanctuary

In 1946 among the property owners whom the County listed in Hillsboro Beach were the following: S.F. Smith Est., H.L. Malcolm, Marie McCollom, Kenneth Parker, J.J. Haggerty, Fred Billing, Three Inc., Ida Flowers, J.A. Rainford, Jeanne Avery, R.J. Slack, J.H. Watty, J.H. Bellick, Margaret Fisher, Glen H. Freidt, Gladys Kalis, P. Parroro, Bill Diesel, Ruth Markland, Ernest Wooler, Charles Russell, Charles Stradella, June Brading, E. Bessey, S. Hillyard, Charles Mount Jr., David Brook, E. Finley, H. Cochran, Vincent Stone, R. Little, James Gavigan, F. Trajton, G. Stradhagen, M. Turton, B. Beatty, A.R. Small, J.W. Spencer, A. Hutner, L. Hendrickson, Harry Bradley, Edward Bradley, Guy Powell, Virginia

Parker Moore, J. Hagerty, J. Sellick, Arthur Wood, Roger Sherman, Charles Russell, D. Brock, O. Dooley, Marion Ponce, L. Timmerman, L. White, L. Leonard, M. Tillotson, W. Harter, C.B. King, D. Sherman, E. Stettinius, Brock and Adelsperger.

Hillsboro Beach remained with its appointed mayor, Allen Malcolm, and its two commissioners for several years. As a town, it was inactive, but as Deerfield Beach began to expand, Hillsboro Beach residents began to feel threatened. Those who had worked so diligently in 1939 to achieve a singular identity for their town did not wish to be annexed by either Deerfield Beach to the north or Pompano Beach to the south. Marie McCollom, a businesswoman who owned the Oceanic Apartments and 14 acres at the north end of town, organized a meeting on February 13, 1947, at the residence of Ruth Markland. Herbert Malcolm called the meeting to order. The group agreed to hold a general election March 4, 1947, from 6:00 to 8:00 P.M. at the Hillsboro Club. Also on the agenda and decided upon that evening were the following items:

1) a paid employee was to be vested with police powers;

2) a zoning commission was to be established;

3) a town commission was to prepare a budget and assess taxes;

4) a town commission was to contact officials of Deerfield Beach and Pompano Beach regarding the distribution of water;

5) McCune, Hiaasen, Fleming and Kelley were retained as corporate counsel.

Little is known about Marie McCollom, the courageous woman who organized the meeting that activated the town of Hillsboro Beach. A letter written on February 22, 1965, by Lynn B. Timmerman of 1212 Hillsboro Beach to Mayor Floyd Grainger, indicates that McCollom was certainly a respected resident of the town.

Dear Floyd:

Since our telephone conversation I have done some research regarding the news article you are preparing. As I understand this feature story regarding Hillsboro Beach is to include not only a history of the Town but its present and past officials. Further that similar write-ups will be made of other towns and cities of Broward County.

Although I was active in the original planning back in the early 40s I do not have very much data to substantiate statements. This much however I am quite positive about: Mrs. Marie R. McCollom of 1223 Hillsboro Beach, is the Mother, Father & Founder of Hillsboro Beach as we know it.

Ernest Wooler, 987 Hillsboro Beach, and first to buy a lot in Hillsboro Mile, was our First Mayor, AND THE ONE PERSON that activated Marie's dreams, and really put our Town in operation, i.e. the Town as we are now known officially. I will qualify the first Mayor statement this much . . . Mr. Smith, at one time owner of most of the first mile, and Mr. Malcolm original owner of the Hillsboro Club, did have some form of an organization called Hillsboro. Mr. Malcolm's nephew carried a title, Mayor.

For factual data may I suggest you contact Mrs. McCollom and Mr. Wooler. I have talked to both about this and am sending them a copy of this letter. I did have some correspondence with Mr. J.F. Riley, Jr., of the Bessemer Corporation of Palm Beach, which company at one time owned most of the oceanfrontage in this section. I cannot locate it now. Thru Mr. Riley, Mrs. McCollom and I secured copies of the Charter and Ordinances of the Town of Gulf Stream (which Bessemer organized). It was upon these papers Marie had our first attorney draw up our Hillsboro organization. I find only one copy of a letter to Marie dated March 2, 1946, regarding 1945 letter.

Ernie Wooler tells me that at one time he prepared an early history of Hillsboro Beach and made it a part of the official records of the village. The Deed and Title of the Town Hall will give data prior to that time. Your minutes will give you all the information since Wooler. All I can do to further this above data would be to eulogize, not only Marie and Ernie, but the many fine men and women who gave so much of themselves and their time to make our present town a reality. This for another time.

Which reminds me that in the not too far distant future we will be ready to celebrate our Silver Anniversary of Hillsboro Beach. It might not be too early now to start collecting pictures, photographs, etc. Right?

Call me if I can be of additional help.

Sincerely,
Lynn

On Thursday, June 16, 1977--twelve years after Timmerman wrote about Marie McCollom in her letter to Mayor Grainger, the *Deerfield Beach Observer* published this obituary of Marie:

PIONEER RESIDENT

MARIE McCOLLOM DIES

Marie R. McCollom, 79, 149 N.E. 18th Avenue, Deerfield Beach, died Tuesday in Winter Haven Fl. Mrs. McCollom has been a pioneer resident of this area since 1940 and was one of the founding City Commissioners of Hillsboro Beach.

She was a member of St. Ambrose Church of Deerfield Beach. She is survived by her daughter Mrs. Arthur B. (Patricia) Schultz of Winter Haven; a brother Jack Robbins of Deerfield Beach and one grandchild. Funeral mass will be said at 10 A.M. today at the St. Ambrose Catholic Church followed by internment in the Boca Raton Cemetery. Contributions may be made to the Boca Community Hospital, in care of the Cancer Research or the building fund of St. Ambrose. Local arrangements by the R. Jay Kraeer Deerfield Beach Funeral Home.

On March 4, 1947, the general election decided upon in the meeting organized by McCollom took place. There were 15 elegible voters, and all 15 cast ballots. Each voter was allowed to vote for three candidates to fill the three-person commission. The votes were:

Ernest Wooler, 14;

Fred Billing, 13;

Herbert L. Malcolm, 13;

Jacob Kalis, 2;

Marie McCollom, 1;

Ruth Markland, 0.

On March 11, 1947, the commission chose Wooler, who had the most votes, to be the first mayor and Malcolm, the vice mayor. Gertrude Wooler was appointed Town Clerk and the remaining officers--zoning commission and committee on assessment and taxation--were appointed by Wooler. A suitable budget, it was suggested, would be $4,500-$5,000, with a salary of $200 a month to be paid to the mayor, plus $100 per month for expenses. The mayor was also to take the place of all hired help for the town. It is extraordinary that a person would devote his life to running a town, but that is what Ernest Wooler did.

Notes and minutes were written by Wooler, who without the help of a typewriter kept all the records for Hillsboro Beach in his own handwriting for the next few years. (See Chapter 9, Subhead: "Ernest Wooler.")

Wooler announced that the reason for "becoming an active township is to avoid the danger of annexation by neighboring municipalities and being subject to their high city taxes and bonded indebtedness." He then proceeded to send letters to all taxpayers and set out to revise the old charter of 1939. This new, revised charter contained the old one practically unaltered, but it was wider in scope in anticipation of future requirements. The Town Charter was granted by the state legislature on June 16, 1947.

When Hillsboro Beach was eight months old, Mayor Wooler wrote this description of his town:

> *Town relatively quiet, little trouble with poachers, signs and barricades were torn down. Policeman Wood (home in Pompano and on Deerfield force) applied for retainer position, but it's not considered necessary at present. Annexation has been avoided for us by Kelley (town Attorney). Taxes would have been 24 mils to start instead of 8 mils for '47. Fifty to 75 feet of the vegetation line moved west . . . South mile wash out 20 feet deep at Hillsboro Club, 15 feet at Stradella's and gradually less than 10 feet at Woolers' and 5 feet at end of mile.*

* * *

The year 1947 brought many changes in the town and consequent challenges for Mayor Wooler. Building permit fees were set at $2 for each $1,000, with a maximum of $50. No trailers were to be permitted to park in town. Numbers assigned to property for convenient reference could be used as house numbers--two numbers were assigned for every 100 feet in width--with odd numbers on the east and even numbers on the west side of the road. Garbage collection was being satisfactorily handled individually by residents.

Building permits had been issued to Malcolm, White, Douchan, Brooks, Stradella (for hurricane repair) and McCollom (for a new building for employees).

By 1948 the town was *on the map*. For some time the town leaders had been concerned not only with water but also with fire protection. Acquiring a fire pumper was not an easy achievement, but it was a top priority. On June 14 the town purchased a red Willys Jeep, Engine No. 543729, for $994.

In his daily notes, Wooler referred to this purchase frequently. He devoted his time and energy to all town problems, but his diary on days surrounding the pumper purchase showed how much his thoughts were on fire protection.

June 3:

Discussed portable fire pump with A.W. Glisson [see Chapter 9, Subhead, "Bill Glisson"] (Bink & Red were caretakers on the mile)--550 gal. per minute pumper--6 cycle Chrysler engine--wants $600. Costs Govt. $1500. but no 4" suction hose . . . Trailer has good tires, etc. also requires accessories, shovels, picks, nozzles etc.

June 6:

Interviewed Fire Chief Ernest Courson and Mayor Blank of Pompano re fire dept. service. Promised prompt service for whole of Hillsboro Beach if called by me or any resident. $25.00 charge for fire truck and 2 men. Each additional volunteer man $5.00 each.

* * *

On June 6, the day Wooler made his notes about the cost of help from the Pompano Fire Department a serious brush fire was reported. Prompt action by the Pompano Fire Department saved the property from being seriously damaged. Kenneth Parker, the property owner on whose land the fire broke out, eventually paid $45 for the aid.

Wooler was definitely the man behind today's contract with local communities for fire protection. If anyone had any doubts about Wooler's daily planning and interest in the development of Hillsboro Beach, one had only to consult his daily dairy.

June 1948 was an eventful month. The town leased from Burwell Smith of York, Pennsylvania, a cottage and garage on 450 feet of property along the intracoastal. The address of the buildings, to be used as a town hall, was: 957, Route #2, Pompano Beach. Route #2 was used by all the residents of the town of Hillsboro Beach as their mailing address, thus Pompano Beach Route #2 was actually Hillsboro Beach.

With the lease of the cottage, the town had its own place for record keeping and conducting business. Meetings continued to be held at the Hillsboro Club or in private homes, since the cottage was too small.

The *Miami Herald* carried an item on July 1, 1951, describing the Hillsboro Beach Town Hall:

SMALLEST CITY HALL AT HILLSBORO BEACH

The smallest city hall in the world, according to Hillsboro Beach City commissioner Benton A. Beatty is in Hillsboro Beach.

He's referring to an 8 by 12 ft. wooden white frame building on Highway A1A in the center of the 16,380-foot long community bordering Pompano Beach at the north.

"We may not have a large building," declared Beatty, "but we have many of the same administration problems that a city like New York, for example, has--only on a smaller scale."

The scale is so much smaller, Beatty admits, that the problems of various departments are housed in separate drawers in a filing cabinet, instead of in separate offices of a big building.

The same man--Amo Angeletti--checks water meters, serves as policeman and fireman, and acts as the town clerk when commissioners meet. Conferences are usually held at a restaurant or club since the building is too small to house Mayor Herbert Malcolm, City Commissioner Mrs. Marie McCollom and Beatty.

A referendum will be held before the summer is over to increase the number of commissioners to five from three. The bill was passed at the last session of the legislature in Tallahassee at the request of the group.

There are 37 homes and eight apartment buildings in Hillsboro Beach, which is 210 feet wide at its narrowest point and 900 feet wide at the widest section.

"We have a completely equipped administration building," Beatty declared pointing to four chairs, a table, typewriters, adding machine and filing cabinet. "All we need is a lie detector and a stenographer."

* * *

As time passed, more permits were issued and more responsibilities were carried by the mayor. The town marshal post, mentioned in the 1951 account above, was approved on November 9, 1948. The marshal was to receive a salary of $150 per month and a house with all utilities furnished. His office was to be at town hall--the cottage--and the garage was to be used for the fire engine. The marshal, according to Wooler's notes, was to act as "sheriff, fire-man, watchman, waterman (meters and bills), road and beach cleaner, bookkeeper for town information, fishing permits, building permits, etc."

On January 4, 1949, Amo Angeletti of the Pompano Beach Police Force was selected as the first person to fill the position of town marshal. (See Chapter 10, " Police Department.")

Wooler stayed continuously busy with conferences and visits to local community officials, seeking a free exchange of ideas for the benefit of the town. He was determined to keep Hillsboro on the map and to establish it as a bona fide community.

Zoning was another prominent issue. Wooler showed up at all new construction sites, offering suggestions and trying to improve and protect the environment. As time passed, the busy mayor saw the passage of ordinances which he actively promoted.

On November 17, 1949, Wooler, in his town meeting notes, wrote the following regarding zoning:

ZONING--Changes, considerable property changes have taken place this summer: French bought the Spencer 125 ft. lot last March and their beautiful new home is practically finished. Bateman sold 150 ft. of his 250 ft. to a Grosse Pointe friend of Mayor Wooler, Lynne Pierson, who anticipates building a home soon. Wellingtons are on the verge of building on 175 feet of their property in the middle of Section 17. P.J.F. Wood of Janesville, Wis. now owns what was Niele Tillotson's 140 feet, and Tillotson now owns 275 feet north of Kenneth Parker, on which he is soon going to build. A Mr. Cannon and his sister, Mrs. Van Court from Memphis, Tenn. purchased 100 feet of the Bateman property north of Shethar. It's the first lot in "B" zoning, and he's drawn up plans to build a Duplex. It's a fortunate gradual change from the residential "A" zoning to the hotel and apartment zoning "B." It is hoped the next north one-half dozen lots will be used for a similar purpose to plan out the Town to the best advantage in the future. Slack's 300 feet at the north end of Town now belongs to a Mr. McDonald of Miami, and is for sale, as is some of Marie McCollom property.

Bateman has made an official request to change "all lands now owned by me and located in Section 17, Township 48, Range 43 E" [to] be zoned Residence "A." Attorney Kelley suggested we get the approval of the property owners 500 feet each side of his property to approve and then put thru the change in Ordinance #2, accordingly, thru the Planning Board. Wellington, with approximately 300 odd feet to the north has already signified his approval as it affects his property also. No difficulty is anticipated as this is from Zoning "B" to "A," not "A" to "B" as is usually the case.

* * *

Wooler, an engineer and a perfectionist by nature, kept copious notes, maps and records, as well as his daily diary. His duties included every issue concerning the town, from revising the charter and handling tax rate complaints and building plans to meeting with Cap to hear his views on civic affairs and dealing with signs to prevent the poaching and shooting of turtles.

Turtle poachers were a constant source of aggravation for the town. Articles referring to the problem frequently appeared in the local news. On May 25 and 27, 1949, there appeared two articles in the *Fort Lauderdale News* and one in the *Miami Herald* regarding the nature and extent of the problem. All three appear below, with the item from the *Herald* appearing last.

UNCOURTEOUS ACTS CAUSED TRESPASS EDICT BY MAYOR

Banning of turtle hunters and other trespassers from the town of Hillsboro Mile, north of Hillsboro Inlet, is the result of a long and continued series of "uncourteous" acts by many of those persons during the last two years, Mayor Ernest Wooler said today [May 25].

Mayor Wooler said many turtle hunters, fishermen, beach party members and others in the past have shown little or no consideration for property owners along the three-mile beach stretch of private property which forms the community.

Five turtles [that were] dragged up the beach last Saturday not only was in violation of game laws, but also was at the expense of damaged foliage planted at appreciable expense by property owners, he said, in pointing out one example.

However, Mayor Wooler said Pompano Beach residents have shown great respect for the private property, and to date, have not violated permits issued to them for surf fishing on the stretch. More than 300 permits requesting no beach fires and that no refuse and litter be left on the beach, have been issued to date by Town Marshal Amo Angeletti.

Mayor Wooler was firm in his declaration that "no further depredations" will be allowed on the legally posted property. He said that persons violating the no trespassing signs on the property will be prosecuted.

The town, formed in 1947, is said to be the longest and most narrow township in the United States. It is owned by some of the nation's outstanding members of financial, political and other fields.

No public roads or rights-of-way open to the public are in the three-mile stretch of private property.

* * *

TURTLE POACHERS OPERATE DESPITE "CLOSED SEASON"

Salt Water Conservation Agent Fred Cabot announced today [May 27] that turtle hunters have been operating off Broward County beaches despite the fact that it is "closed season" on the huge sea turtles.

Fort Lauderdale and Hillsboro police on Thursday spotted a boat which was sending a man with a rope ashore to tow the big reptiles out to sea as they were attempting to lay eggs in the sands, Cabot said. He declared that, although the occupants of this particular boat escaped, a close watch will be kept in the future.

He explained that possession of turtles or eggs between May 1 and Aug. 31 is punishable by a fine not to exceed $500 with the eggs protected an additional 30 days.

It is during this period that the huge sea turtles, weighing up to 600 pounds, crawl out on the beach to scrape out a shallow hole in which more than 100 eggs are laid before the turtle covers the eggs with sand and crawls back to the water.

The heat of the sun hatches the eggs and the young turtles, in turn, also crawl down to the sea.

While on the beach, the turtles are utterly helpless and can be prized over on their backs by use of a pole, to be butchered at leisure by lawless hunters.

Cabot said that a sharp lookout by all county law enforcement agents as well as by himself, has been promised and that any person found in possession of turtles or eggs will be prosecuted.

* * *

TURTLE HUNTS STIR WRATH AT HILLSBORO

[May 27] Trespassers and turtle hunters have

been ordered not to enter the town of Hillsboro, north of the Hillsboro Inlet, following a series of "uncourteous" acts during the past two years, Mayor Ernest Wooler reported yesterday.

No consideration for property owners along the three-mile stretch of private beach which forms the community has been shown by fishermen, beach party members and turtle hunters, Mayor Wooler said.

* * *

For Mayor Wooler, who was an active member of the Audubon Society, nature was a prime passion, along with caring for the town. The National Audubon Society and its Florida affiliate were founded at the turn of the century. The near extermination of beautiful plume birds, American and snowy egrets, sparked the organization and provided an immediate cause for the Florida organization to champion. Despite adversity and tragedies, such as the death of two wardens, the society's wardens steadfastly patrolled vast areas to protect the state's wildlife, even in the remote stretches of Florida wilderness.

By November 1949, 400-500 permits for fishing had been issued; many were for fishing at the Blue Fish Hole, located just south of The Barefoot Mailman Restaurant. Twenty arrests were made that year for poaching and disorderly conduct.

Turtle abuses have been reported throughout the town's history. Today the Hillsboro Club, cooperating with Broward County, Nova University and the Florida Environmental Protection Program, promotes the protection of Florida's sea turtles. Abuses have diminished greatly since Mayor Wooler's confrontations with the trespassers and abusers of the Hillsboro Beach homeowners' properties.

Second Decade: The '50s

For three years Wooler was tireless in his efforts for the town and for the environment, two causes which, for him, went hand in hand. There were other forces at work in the small town, however, and not everyone agreed with the mayor's opinions. In March 1950, in a letter to Malcolm, who was on vacation in Mexico, Wooler revealed both his frustration and his determination to press on:

> *Dear Bert:*
>
> *Enclosed please find the Minutes of the March 14th commissioners' meeting. Because of your absence, the meeting ended in a deadlock, not only for the appointment of Mayor, but for the appointment of all other officers as well. It is just as well it did as all subjects are too important to the Town to be decided without all three of the newly elected commissioners getting together. We must get started again and try to hold our Town together for another three years, at least.*
>
> *I was quite concerned when we hadn't heard from you after all the telegrams and letters I sent, but I understand you talked to Bill Kelley just before the meeting.*
>
> *It was quite an affair--twenty-five people. Only half could get inside our tiny Town Hall. Then the rain came!-- about the middle of it all. We closed up the chairs, and wedged them in, all standing up. However, we managed. Some day my plan for improving and remodeling the buildings we were so fortunate to get from Smith may go through--if we can get together again in one congenial group. Right now there is still a bickering half dozen, who are sulking.*
>
> *Kalis held the floor most of the meeting with typical, well shall I say, persistence. This Town is*

made up of people of the highest type. It seems a pity that it should be wrecked by a mere half dozen. John White attended and appears to be giving his moral support to the Mal-contents.

Bill Kelley and others spoke long and seriously of the disaster that awaits us as a town if the bickering does not stop.

Laws were passed at the last State legislature making it impossible to incorporate a town which has less than three hundred population. If we cannot agree among ourselves, our little Town will dissolve like smoke. By the way, the few who are causing the trouble were there in force. None of our people, who should be vitally interested, were there except Roger Sherman and Rainford.

When you return we will hold our next meeting, and swear you in as commissioner. If you nominate me for Mayor, I shall try to hold the town together and serve as best I can for another three years.

I am appointed as delegate to the District Conference of the Power Squadron in Tampa on April 1-2. [Wooler had been elected Lieutenant Commander of the Fort Lauderdale Power Squadron.] Gert and I may be away for a long weekend. However, if you return April 1st, I shall be back for a meeting on April 3rd.

With best regards to you and Pat, I remain,

Sincerely,
Ernest

Clearly Wooler wished to remain as mayor, but his letter did not elicit the response he expected from his friend Malcolm. With the best interests of the town in mind, Malcolm gave great weight to the dissension among the other residents. As diplomatically as he could, he explained his thinking to Wooler:

Fri. 24 March 1950

Dear Ernest,

I quite agree with you that you are by far the best man for mayor, but am not sure that it is wise for you to have the office, if we thereby wreck the town by throwing the present squabbles into active war and disruption. Before supporting you for mayor, I must assure myself by a personal canvas of the situation that the trouble makers cannot and will not break up the town, if you are mayor. . . . I do not want the position, but I do not believe any of us want the town to break up. I will go into this with you as soon as I get back on April 3rd. . . .

Sincerely,
Bert Malcolm

Elections were held on March 14, 1950. Of the 38 persons who were registered, 36 cast ballots. The results:

H. Malcolm, 33
E. Wooler, 24
M. McCollom, 16
B. Beatty, 15

Malcolm was chosen as mayor and Marie McCollom as vice mayor. Amo Angeletti was reinstated as town clerk, inspector of buildings, town marshal and all other appointive offices, including tax assessor and collector. His salary was increased to $180 per month. C.C. Radcliff of Pompano Beach served as Judge of the Municipal Court, and court costs were fixed at a minimum of $3 per case.

In 1949 Mayor Wooler had requested permission to trade in his Studebaker to purchase a new car, suitable for police work, out of his own pocket and operated at his own expense. The town was to pay insurance and license fees. Finally in May 1950, the town approved the purchase of a police car with radio.

In September 1950, Burwell Smith gave notice that he would cancel the lease with Hillsboro Beach for his cottage and garage, stating that he had "listed said lands for sale." They would be sold later to William Farrell for $600. Now, added to other issues, there was an increased impetus to build a new town hall, a long-held goal of former Mayor Wooler. Commissioners continued to use the Smith property.

With the election of 1950, discord among town residents seemed to lessen and bickering decreased. Some friction, however, was inevitable, for even in a tiny hamlet in the '50s, the role of government was an issue. Individuals disagreed over their government's role in controlling construction, water use and beach erosion. (See Chapter 12, "Hurricanes and Erosion.") Another matter that stirred heated discussion was the question of a post office, but town officials found no solution. Records for 1950 show that taxes collected for that year amounted to $10,567.43.

In other business, a motion by Malcolm was passed instructing the town attorney to prepare an amendment to the town charter, resolving that there be five commissioners instead of three, with alternating terms, so that an election could be held every spring, and the term of office be two years; that the town be authorized to enter into franchises with public utilities; that there be provision for attendance at town meetings by town committees; that additional powers be given to the town commission, including authorization to levy a utility service tax subject to approval by referendum of the registered voters of the town. The resolution further provided that all of the foregoing changes be first approved by a referendum by the qualified electors of the town of Hillsboro Beach.

The amendment, titled House Bill No. 437, was passed by the state legislature that year.

On October 8, 1951, the town acquired a new mailing address: Route 2, Box 960, Pompano, Florida. A1A had been paved in 1941. Now, ten years later, the town put in a request to the state for lights at both ends of town. The request was denied, but two town identification signs were installed, one at each end of town.

Water problems continued to plague the town, with water being cut off for hours without first notifying the residents. The situation demanded attention by town officials. A well site on Sample Road was considered and later acquired. Out of 26 registered freeholders, 24 voted in favor of the water bonds.

In 1952, G. Russell French and Anne Cannon were sworn in as commissioners. (Elisha Cannon, A.D. Henderson, and Benton A. Beatty had been sworn in as commissioners in 1951, in accordance with the new charter.) Ernest Wooler had removed himself from the commission in order to help achieve harmony in the town. Regular meetings were established on the first Tuesday of each month at 10 A.M., and all committees were to submit written reports.

Matters which came before the commission included: the approval of Charles Kanode Jr. of the U.S. Coast Guard to serve as a town patrolman with a salary of $200 per month; a public hearing to grant a 30-year franchise to Florida Power and Light (leading to an ordinance to that effect); and a discussion dealing with the matter of regulating the bridge openings at the inlet, which were causing tremendous traffic jams.

In 1952 the voters list for the town of Hillsboro Beach was made up of the following names: Amendola, Nina; Amendola, Thomas; Angeletti, Evelyn; Angeletti, Amo; Bateman, Elizabeth; Bateman, Robert; Beatty, Benton; Beatty, Juliette; Beatty, Minnie; Benson, T.R.; Benson, Marguerite; Billing, Marjorie; Billing, Fred; Burke, Alan;

Burke, Augusta; Cannon, Annie; Carpenter, Henry; French, Frances; French, George Sr.; French, George Jr.; Glisson, Arthur W.; Glisson, Geneveve; Hayes, Archie; Hardeman, Thomas; Henderson, Alexander; Henderson, Lucy; Hobbs, John; Hobbs, Rita; Isler, Luther; Isler, Ruth; Kelley, Richard; King, C.B.; King, __; Loughead, Ruth; Malcolm, Herbert; Malcolm, Patricia; Markland, Ruth Purdy; McCollom, Marie; McCollom, Patricia; MacDonald, Emiley; MacDonald, Howard; Neaville, Frank; Neaville, Mary Jane; Orvis, Rhoda; Pancoast, Martha; Pancoast, Norman; Sauer, Miriam; Schlangen, __; Schlangen, __; Seymour, Virginia; Small, __; Small, __; Van Arsdale, __; Van Arsdale, __; Van Court, Bernice; Wood, Lucille; Wooler, Ernest; Wooler, Gertrude; Weaver, George; Weaver, Lula.

By January 1953 the water distribution system was fully in operation from the new water field on Sample Road. Russell French was again re-elected to serve as mayor for another two years. The year was an active one. Roy Glisson was contracted at $3600 a year for by-weekly collection of garbage. Harland Bartholomew and Associates, City Planners and Civil Engineers of St. Louis, Missouri, were retained to help with town planning and revising zoning and new ordinances. Signs were placed at the town limits in the Intracoastal Waterway "warning all boatmen to operate boats with no wash or wake which may cause damage to property."

The ever-present problems with the inlet bridge occupied much of the commissioners' time again in 1953. In discussions about building a new bridge, concerns about detriment to the surrounding properties were aired.

The town benefited that year from actions made by utility companies. Southern Bell converted the telephone exchange from Pompano to an extended scope of service with a new phone number, WH 1-4009. Florida Power and Light announced that they would install new lights in town.

Vice Mayor Elisha Cannon passed away in 1953, and in tribute to his efforts as a commissioner toward establishing the water field on Sample, it was decided that the commissioners' room in the new town hall would be named Cannon Hall. Plans for the building continued.

World War II had reinvigorated Hillsboro Beach, the southeast coast and all of Florida. Highway and airport construction had accelerated, so that by the '50s Florida had an up-to-date transportation network for the endless caravan of tourists. Tourism, cattle, citrus and phosphate remained extremely important to Florida's economy, and new industries created many new jobs. While space exploration begun in that decade may be the most outstanding mark of progress, there were also innovations in electronics, plastics, forest products, construction, real estate and international finance.

Increasingly the southern east coast had become a force to reckon with. In 1944 J. Myer Schine, a Latvian immigrant who had come to America penniless, at the age of 11, purchased the Boca Raton Club for $3 million. When the club had been taken over by the federal government to house military personnel in 1942, troops quartered there called it the most elegant barracks of all time. When Schine bought the property, the town of Boca Raton was little more than a hamlet. As elsewhere in Florida, however, progress was inevitable.

In 1955 Schine announced his intention to make Boca Raton "the most beautiful spot on the Gold Coast," and he began a $1 million shopping center on 25 acres as part of his plan. In 1956 Arthur Vining Davis would buy the Boca Raton Hotel and Club from Schine for $22.5 million, at that time the biggest real estate deal in Florida history.

Progress also found Pompano Beach. With a boost in its economy during the war, its population began to grow. By 1940 the town had 4,427 residents. Within a three-mile range south of the Hillsboro Mile, Pompano had 250 buildings valued at $3 million. The southern border of the area was about one mile south of the Pompano Beach Bathing Casino and Dance Hall.

As with other loosely defined residential localities in southeast Florida, the issue of organization versus individual sovereignty had been a hot topic around Pompano for years. Finally in 1947, the matter of consolidating Pompano, Pompano Beach and Oceanway Park--"a track of no-man's land" (according to Pompano's anniversary booklet) which lay between the two townships--was settled in 1947 with the formation of the city of Pompano Beach. Tying the area together were the Kester cottages, which lined the beach, and the streets of Old Pompano (NE 11th and 13th Avenues and First Street). The farmers of Old Pompano and the resort residents of east Federal Highway were united in the 1960s by the widening of Atlantic Boulevard between Federal Highway and the railroad tracks. In 1948 the Pompano Beach Chamber of Commerce was organized.

That same year, in January, a fire broke out in a boathouse adjacent to Cap's Place. The fire was fought in a bucket brigade fashion, and even though the fire-fighters were there quickly, three skiffs and four small rowboats, which had been used to transport Cap's patrons, were destroyed.

By 1949 the city of Pompano Beach had launched a project to maintain and improve the navigability of the Hillsboro Inlet. The project netted $146,000 in expenditures, but these costs were met in part by private contributors who knew that fishing at the inlet helped boost the tourist industry. Pompano civic leader Roland Hardy remembered: "Fishing was always good around the Hillsboro Inlet. Once I saw a crew of a fishing boat net 100,000 pounds of mullet in less than a day."

Pompano, in 1950, had a population of 4,682, telephone connections numbering 912, a public school enrollment of 2,209 students and a newspaper, the *Town News*. By 1959 the building boom had sent permit values soaring to a total of $16 million in Pompano Beach.

In Hillsboro Beach, problems stemming from progress continued to plague city commissioners. Traffic had increased tremendously, and two policemen were hired on a temporary basis. With an influx of families with young children, there arose a need for educational facilities. In 1955 Alexander Henderson petitioned the town to build a private elementary school, which was later built at the north end of town and called the Hillsboro Country Day School. (See Chapter 9, Subhead: Alexander Henderson.")

Also in 1955, Thaddeus R. Benson was nominated mayor; Nicholas Schlangen and Alexander Henderson were tied for vice mayor. A coin was flipped and the nomination went to Henderson.

On March 17, 1955, an open house--at last--was held in the new town hall. Mrs. Elisha Cannon accepted the plaque honoring her husband. The new location was at 1210 Hillsboro Mile. Ruth Purdy Markland, chairman of the beautification committee, gave her final report, and the new town hall became Hillsboro Beach's new home.

Changes were again made in the charter. As the town grew, so did the need for new revisions. In June 1955 a resolution was passed to "adopt the building code of the City of Fort Lauderdale, to be the building code of the town of Hillsboro Beach."

In September of that year, citing pressure and too

many responsibilities, Amo Angeletti resigned. George Garland became the new town marshal.

In 1956, 50 of the 59 registered voters in Hillsboro Beach voted, electing T. Benson as mayor and A. Henderson as vice mayor. Later in the month of the election, Benson passed away, and Henderson became mayor. Commissioner Schlangen was appointed vice mayor and Frank Neaville was appointed to fill Benson's term. Ethel Grant was appointed as Town Clerk.

The first liquor license in Hillsboro was granted to The Barefoot Mailman Hotel on October 10, 1956. The second license would not be awarded for three years, going to Florida Hillsboro, Inc., on November 11, 1959.

Elections were held on February 28, 1957. Seventy-two of the 74 registered voters cast their votes. The clerk of election and the inspectors of election received $1.50 for their services. Anne Cannon and Allen Reid were administered the oath of office as new commissioners and also took the non-Communist oath. Henderson was reappointed mayor. In order to bring the town's fiscal year closer to the date of the county assessment valuations, the fiscal year was changed to begin on May 1 and end the following April 30.

That year municipality employees were covered under social security laws, and Hillsboro Beach became a member of the Broward County League of Municipalities, paying dues of $25.

Ordinances passed by the Hillsboro Beach Commissioners in 1957 were designed to regulate signs, licenses and fees. The new laws controlled the erection of signs, billboards and awnings; set a schedule of fees for sign permits; regulated speed for vehicles; prohibited and authorized punishment for any act within the town limits which was recognized by the laws of Florida as a misdemeanor;

and established regulations for the application of licenses and the setting of expiration dates and fees.

That same year George Garland resigned as town marshal, being replaced by Raymond T. McMullin. Commissioner Herbert Malcolm also resigned, and Clint B. King was appointed to replace him. In another personnel measure taken in 1957, Holiday Landscaping and Maintenance Company won the bid for garbage removal for $14,995. Allen K. Reid and Ann Cannon were appointed to represent Hillsboro Beach on the committee regarding the proposed new bridge over Hillsboro Inlet.

In the 1959 elections, Alexander Henderson was again nominated as mayor, and Robert Bateman was appointed to replace Glisson on the Hillsboro Inlet Commission. (Bateman resigned the following year and was replaced by Baird Tewksbury Jr.) Also in 1959, bids were opened for building an additional garage to house the fire truck.

Third Decade: The '60s

In 1960 Allen K. Reid resigned as commissioner after selling his property at 1165 Hillsboro Mile. He was replaced by Benton A. Beatty. Henderson was again nominated as mayor, his term to run until 1964. He was the longest serving mayor of Hillsboro Beach, having been nominated for nine consecutive years.

In 1961 Hillsboro Beach began displaying auto decals, perhaps the least controversial action to be seen in the little town in the decade. The '60s brought two very sensitive issues to the small town: 1) the question of whether a new bridge was needed at the Hillsboro Inlet and 2) the county's proposed acquisition of beach frontage for public use. These matters became prime concerns for all of the town's residents, and they were not resolved until 1966 for the bridge and 1967 for the beach issue.

Ernest Wooler strenuously opposed the building of a new bridge at the south end of town. In his notes, as President of the Hillsboro Inlet Improvement Association, he listed his reasons:

1. Not an Intracoastal water-way bridge.

2. Money saved can be used for other purposes--such as right-of-way for Pompano new four lane bridge.

3. Bridge now being electrified which will reduce opening and closing time from 8 min. to 5 min. and save manual labor.

4. Road approach is only about 20 feet wide.

5. All people on both sides strenuously object to widening road and don't want to sell right of way.

6. Bridge controls necessary speed of traffic at this point, 16 feet wide, as hundreds of people gather on south

7. [sic] side of bridge to watch charter boats come and go.

8. Bridge only used by pleasure craft no commercial boats.

9. Bridge in fairly good condition, only needs foot walks on each side.

10. No need for higher or wider bridge at this time, as no traffic delay except to open and close a few times each day.

Despite Wooler's efforts, February 24, 1965, was "moving day." The bridge was disassembled in pieces, moved to its temporary spot beside the new construction, and reinstalled for use until the new span was built. Condemnation action on property needed for the bridge to get rights-of-way and detour routes were filed against Hillsboro Association, Inc., the Yardarm Restaurant, and Hillsboro Inlet Docks. The cost of construction was estimated at $750,000.

Two articles appeared regarding completion of the bridge in the *Fort Lauderdale Sun-Sentinel*, the first on April 27, 1966, the day before the opening, and the second on April 29, the day after:

WE'LL CROSS BRIDGE WHEN "IT" GETS HERE

Yards of cement, tons of steel, hundreds of man-hours of labor and nearly $1 million have gone into the Hillsboro Inlet bridge, and work is now completed with a formal ribbon cutting ceremony set for Thursday at 11:30 A.M.

There will be dignitaries, bands, photographers, newsmen and all the hoopla which attends such events. But there may be a slight problem. Or rather, there may be a slight piece of equipment which will cause a major problem. Without it, the bridge will not be able to provide its primary function--carry traffic across the inlet while opening periodically to permit boats to go down to the sea or home from it.

A small condenser, one of those intricate little things that goof up the television, mess up the car motor or cause trouble in many electrical devices, went on the blink at the bridge.

Turning to another of man's electronic creations, a call went out to New York for a replacement. And still another fantastic invention, the airplane, was called upon to deliver the replacement part. But, alas, it appears that the most devious of man's inventions, the delivery schedule, has gone awry.

And so it will happen, Thursday, unless the little condenser has better luck than some misplaced baggage has a habit of doing. After all the ceremony is completed, it will only be possible to cross the bridge with a pogo-stick. It seems that condenser is necessary to close the bridge for the last few inches.

* * *

BRIDGE OPENS . . . WELL ALMOST

[Pompano] Mayor Stewart Kester proposed Thursday that the new Hillsboro Inlet Bridge be named in honor of Alex Henderson, formal mayor of Hillsboro Beach, "who worked so long and hard to have it built."

Kester spoke briefly at the official ribbon-cutting ceremony, held midway on the bridge at 11:30 A.M. State Road Board member Chelsea Senerchia made the actual ribbon cut, with an able assist from Linda Hanson, Miss Pompano Beach.

City officials did not miss the opportunity to immediately suggest to Senerchia they hope to see him back on the same type of mission next year, opening the 14th Street Bridge.

There were bands, politicians, spectators and just about everything to attend the bridge opening. All that was missing were those little diodes needed to close the bridge so traffic can roll across it.

Mayor Arthur Wood of Hillsboro Beach represented his community at the event. He observed that "the state and county may think this is their bridge, but we know it belongs to Hillsboro Beach and Pompano Beach." With a smile, he declared, "it should be painted red and blue, with the blue on our side since ours is the prettiest."

The draw span operates to open on the south side, and five diodes, which cost a total of some $26 are keeping the bridge inoperative for vehicular traffic. The parts are supposed to have been sent via plane from a plant in Virginia, but appear to have *gone astray. Until they arrive and are installed, only boat traffic through the inlet will be moving.*

A luncheon was held at the Yardarm Restaurant following the opening, which was not an opening. When the diodes arrive, they will be installed and local residents will probably plan their own observation, and the hero is expected to be the fellow who pushes the button which finally crops the span into crossing position.

* * *

In 1963 Hillsboro Beach reported 94 registered voters and tremendous beach erosion, the greatest since 1947. Also in that year, the town launched an all-out battle to prevent acquisition of beach property by the county for public bathing and recreation.

Out of six locations which the county had chosen for acquisition, two were selected in Hillsboro Beach. One of the two sites was an 870-foot area south of Virginia Kay Apartments and north of the Monterey House. The other was a 650-foot stretch north of the Hillsboro Mile Apartments. The Area Planning Board (APB) had recommended parking facilities for cars on both sides of A1A.

"We don't want it and I don't think the area is suitable," Mayor Henderson declared. "We have a little town and it doesn't even lend itself to it--there's not even a taxi stand here. We have no streets--we don't want any. With the narrow highway, we already have enough traffic problems."

In order to get a response from the people, Henderson said nearly 500 questionnaires would be sent out. Hillsboro Beach resident Floyd Grainger, who would later succeed Henderson as mayor, said that public beaches would devalue property by two-thirds and recommended to the Broward County Commission that they pay residents in Hillsboro Beach for the devaluation. Grainger insisted that public beaches would violate all zoning restrictions in the town.

An angry delegation of residents appeared at the hearing of the APB. None of the 470 residents who answered the questionnaire favored the beach proposal, and others expressed a desire to assume the share of any expense involved in litigation.

Henderson had pledged to "give them the damnedest fight they ever saw. This is a nice little community--one of the prettiest in Florida--and we can do without any public beaches to spoil it." There was no need for a fight. The APB chose not to accept the two sites in Hillsboro Beach.

Construction continued at a steady pace throughout the town. On April 21, 1967, in the Sun-Sentinel, an article by Sydney Magill appeared. It best describes the building trend of the times:

NO BUILDING IN HILLSBORO?

Hillsboro Beach, one of the most picturesque communities in South Florida, is waging a battle to preserve its image as a quiet community of oceanfront homesites with a minimum of intrusion from the influx of high-risers.

Its residents have historically opposed co-operative and high-rise construction, but several have been built and started. The high-risers approved have met the strict codes during the past few years and two more are being considered for zoning and design requirements set up to retain the atmosphere of the community which is located north of Pompano Beach between the Intracoastal Waterway and the ocean.

In an apparent effort to keep developers out, the town does not release monthly or annual valuations of building permits. Month after month, it shrugs off value of new construction as "zero."

"Write us a letter and we will take it up at a council meeting," Commissioner and former Mayor Arthur Wood declared when queried about the unusual practice. Wood said there is virtually no new construction going on in the community, whose only thoroughfare is SR A1A.

Failure to list construction gives potential developers the impression that there is no building in the community. However, it also makes it difficult to provide actual totals of building and construction valuations in Broward County. Other communities may share similar views on high-risers, but they make no attempt to hide them.

New construction was frowned upon when the community was established 20 years ago, but many residents now have a more liberal view on building and development. They feel that if it is orderly and the architecture in keeping with the atmosphere of the community it should be acceptable.

Regulations are in force which define the setback lines, the number of parking spaces and other factors relevant to construction. The high-risers which have been built and are now being started have underground parking so as not to clutter up the grounds with parked vehicles.

* * *

In 1964 Mayor Grainger wrote in a newsletter to the town residents:

> *The grounds and buildings of the Town Hall are being kept in excellent condition and we are having the Town Hall Commission Room equipped with storm shutters so that the room may be used at any time during storms as a shelter. This room may be*

used by bonafide organizations within our Town at no cost to same. Also, we are purchasing a standby power generator in the event of any electric power failure.

All buildings under construction are daily checked by our qualified building inspector in strict accordance with the adopted South Florida Building Code. Our inspector also checks on all licenses and permits issued in the Town.

For the convenience of the residents of the Town, we are awaiting word from the Postal Authorities on the requested Post Office station to be operated at the Town Hall. We have also requested that a large Drop-In Mail Box be erected on the grounds of the Town Hall instead of the small mail box now located across the street.

The town commissioners later agreed not to have a postal station.

In 1964 Margaret Froedge replaced Ethel Grant as Town Clerk. Mayor Henderson passed away and was replaced by Floyd Grainger. Town Attorney Clarke continued making changes in the town charter.

In April 1969 Attorney Clarke presented the new charter changes to the state legislature. In his letter to the Honorable Chester W. Stolzenburg, Clarke summarized the changes being made:

The Bill presented to you represents no significant change in either organization, administration or election of the Town officials. The form of government remains the same.

Under Article III the powers of the Town are more definitely delineated than they have been in previous Charters and Charter of the Town is brought more closely in accord with the general

Statutes of the State of Florida with regard to financing, zoning and so forth, as evidenced by Article III, Section 7, page 7, and Article III Sections 39, 40 and 41, page 32.

The one substantial power that has never been granted to the Town heretofore is that set forth in Article III, Section 21, under the heading of Beach Erosion. Although Hillsboro Beach is incorporated in the Broward County Beach Erosion District, they have received no help or assistance from Broward County and have received no return on property taxes paid to the Broward County Beach Erosion District because all of the beaches of Hillsboro Beach are private property; each lot or tract of land runs from the Intra-Coastal Waterway to the Atlantic Ocean with reparian and littoral rights vested in the individual owners. This being the case, in this Charter the same beach erosion authority has been set forth for the Town as that that has been created for the Town of Jupiter and Hobe Sound. They have made no attempt to withdraw from the Broward County Beach Erosion District but since they have gotten no relief from that legislation and can expect none, they have asked for legislative machinery to combat beach erosion within their own Town limits and Article III, Section 21, is patterned exactly after the beach erosion legislation that has heretofore been passed for the Towns enumerated above.

More attention is paid in this Charter to the financial rules and regulations of the Town as set forth in Article V which basically represents the same rules and regulations under which the City of Lighthouse Point operates and the details and restrictions are similar to many other towns in the area. The prior charter of the Town and supplement was silent on the matter.

Article VII, page 62, sets forth a more direct chain of command for the Police and Fire Departments than was contained in any prior Charter and a prior Bill which gave the Town Police the right to make arrests in "fresh pursuit" anywhere within Broward County, Florida, is now incorporated in Article VII, Section 1, page 64.

Other than these changes, the Charter has been approved and submitted simply because it is a better, more comprehensive Charter than anything that the Town of Hillsboro Beach had heretofore. It contains nothing controversial and there are no "sleepers." It merely represents an effort on the part of the Town of Hillsboro Beach to overhaul its own internal rules and procedures.

Very truly yours,
Clarke and O'Brien
Russell B. Clarke

* * *

The new changes in the Charter passed in May 1969. The new Erosion Committee, now under the new Charter, consisted of Chairman D. Winton, F. Garman and E. Williams.

On Sunday, April 21, 1963, the *Miami Herald* published an article which clearly summarized the sentiment which characterized Hillsboro Beach throughout the '60s.

HILLSBORO BEACH SAYS: STAY OUT
TOWN DOESN'T HAVE A STORE . . .
NOT EVEN A TAXI STAND

It is significant that the only direct county tax benefit accruing to the town Hillsboro Beach yearly is the pickup and delivery of four city children by school bus.

For this academic service, the town pays Broward County some $60,000 annually in tax dollars and no one complains too loudly about doing it.

Or, at least, none of the city's 88 registered voters has refused to pay the taxes for the limited return.

Hillsboro People are mostly part-time residents who live in the cooperative apartments or vacation homes along its 3.4 mile beach.

And civic calm is threatened not so much by taxes, but by invasions of privacy like the tentative county annexation of 1,520 feet of town property for use as a public beach . . .

Hillsboro Beach is pretty. It is only 900 feet from side to side--the ocean to the Intracoastal Waterway--at its widest point.

Its main street is State Road A1A. There are no others. Its southern half is made up of luxury homes hidden from the gaze of passing motorists by thick trees and dense shrubbery.

Along the northern half of main street are the handsome co-ops, its lone hotel, The Barefoot Mailman, and a handful of motels.

There are no stores, "not even a taxi-stand," said Mayor Henderson. "The town was formed in 1947 by a few of us," he said, "and nobody has ever particularly wanted any." It has a four-man police force, a fire department, and five town commissioners. The mayor said the civic officials receive no salary: "It's all for free . . ."

Most of the town's year-round population of 500 is made up of retirees--peaceful people who take great delight in doing nothing more strenuous than sunning on the all-private beaches, gardening, puttering around pitch-and-putt greens or fishing on the intracoastal.

The pace picks up in December when the winter population swells to around 2,000. Then begin the co-op parties and the Sunday golf tournaments. The traffic through the city's 35-mile-an-hour zones along A1A is slow-moving. Tempers blaze when the old inlet bridge is "up" and traffic stacks up.

And often oldtime residents wish for the days only 16 years ago when Hillsboro Beach was incorporated with just six homes on its beach.

* * *

By the end of 1969, Hillsboro boasted 309 voters. One hundred were freeholders. The commission that year asked residents to correct the "overdense shrubbery and trees along A1A which extend into and over the highway, [and which] are an eyesore and traffic hazard, hiding driveways and road signs."

Arthur R. Wood had followed Mayor Floyd Grainger as mayor in 1966. Anne Rode won the position in 1967, Christian Truelson in 1968 and Charles Stradella in 1969. At the end of the decade, in 1970, William Stuart was elected mayor.

Fourth Decade: The '70s

During Mayor Stuart's administration the town was concerned with many of the same problems as those faced by the past several administrations. News letters were periodically sent to the residents to keep them informed of the problems and the progress made in solving them. Both the Erosion Committee and the Zoning Board were always very active. Mayor Stradella had felt a lack of communication between the town officials and the co-ops and condominiums, and had suggested a committee to serve as their representative.

The decade of the 1970s was not only busier than any earlier period, it also saw more controversy. Arguments regarding all of the issues of the time--erosion, annexation, zoning, sewers and politics--rose to a frenzied pitch. In 1961, Walt Disney World had opened near Orlando, attracting more people each year than Florida had permanent residents. Hillsboro Beach felt the impact.

The census for Hillsboro Beach in 1970 recorded 1,181 residents for the town and 532 registered voters. In council business, the Florida Retirement Plan (a cooperative effort between the state and the town) was adopted, no-parking signs were placed along A1A, Opal Towers was nearly completed, Town Clerk Margaret Froedge resigned, and the Broward County Governmental Efficiency Study Committee proposed that the town be annexed by Pompano Beach.

Another matter in 1970 was the question of the county's jurisdiction over the town. During one town council meeting, there was discussion about enacting an ordinance which would make ineffective all county ordinances which conflicted with the town's laws. The town's attorney, Russell Clarke, issued a stinging attack against the county government. He believed the county to be guilty of passing ordinances with the goal of abolishing municipal government. Hillsboro commissioners, as well as leaders of other local municipalities, wanted to take immediate action.

Fire protection was an issue that had carried over from the '60s. In 1969, a tri-city fire station--serving Boca Raton, Deerfield Beach and Hillsboro Beach--had been proposed to protect beach property. Because of the distance between the three towns, the suggestion had been tabled. Deerfield fire fighters responded to Hillsboro alarms until the Pompano Highlands force contracted to do so in 1967. Fire calls were scarce, however, since

Hillsboro's Police Department handled minor fires.

Still, it became increasingly clear that Hillsboro needed more reliable protection, and residents pressed for their own fire truck. By 1970, Deerfield Beach and Pompano were placing a truck on the beach side of the intracoastal every time the bridge was repaired. A fire contract with the Pompano Beach Highlands Volunteer Department was signed in November 1972 for one year, at a cost of $13,000.

On March 2, 1971, Hillsboro Beach voters were presented with a bond issue for restoration and protection of the beaches. The issue, which passed, was set at $800,000. An estimated $500,000 was to be spent on the first phase of sand replenishment. The remaining amount could be used for construction of groins or for annual nourishment, depending on the future rate of erosion to the beaches. (See Chapter 12, "Hurricanes and Erosion.")

A perennial topic for the town was zoning. In February 1972, the matter sent tempers flaring at Town Hall as the commissioners wrestled with revisions to proposed zoning ordinances. The debate centered on a proposal to allow only three-story dwellings to be erected in areas not included in two previously specified "hi-rise" areas. One of these ran from Opal Towers Apartments north to the Hillsboro Windsor. The other area ran south from Ocean Hillsboro to the Landmark Apartments. In these high-rise areas, seven-story buildings were allowed east of A1A; only three stories were permitted on the west side.

During the discussion, Mayor Erickson announced that the zoning proposals had met with the approval of Professor Claude Polk of the University of Miami. An expert in town zoning, Polk had accepted an invitation to come to town to discuss the new zoning restrictions in the near future.

City attorney Russell Clarke was annoyed at the announcement. "If you men desire the legal services of 'outsiders'," he said, "I am willing to resign as city attorney." Further, he charged the commissioners with "evading responsibility and depending on outsiders to make your decisions for you."

The zoning debate continued over the next few months. There were two major aspects for discussion. Paramount was the question of density, but land use was also a factor. As residents took sides, one landowner threatened to donate his land to a church rather than develop it under existing density restrictions.

Other landowners complicated the issue with their attitude. Sam Ferguson of Boca Raton and Paul Kelsey of Delray Beach allowed their stretches of beach to be used by the public. Other owners complained about the practice, since stragglers often wandered from the Ferguson and Kelsey properties onto the beaches that were not public. Residents of Hillsboro preferred that their community be one for residents rather than transients, but the town's commissioners could do nothing about the complaints against Ferguson and Kelsey. The two men were within their legal rights.

Work on the zoning ordinance continued. Three months after Attorney Clarke offered to resign over an outsider's being invited in to give counsel, he angrily quit during a commission meeting (May 1972). He nearly walked out. The matter which precipitated Clarke's sudden resignation was the order in which items on the agenda were to be discussed. The third reading of the controversial zoning change was set to be heard and voted upon before City Engineer Arthur Stock's report, which that day concerned The Barefoot Mailman property. Normally, Strock's report followed the approval of the previous meeting's minutes, but on this agenda, the final vote on the zoning ordinance had been scheduled immediately after the reading of the minutes.

Clarke took issue with this, since passage of the ordinance would make any action concerning The Barefoot Mailman property irrelevant. Palm-Aire Corporation had plans to erect a ten-story condominium at the site of their property, but if the new ordinance passed before the plan was submitted, the ten-story building would be illegal without any discussion.

When the commissioners agreed to change the order in which the matters would be discussed, Clarke revised the effective date of his resignation from "immediately" to the end of May. In other commission business that month, the council voted to set aside $1,000 for repair of the sea wall abutting town hall property.

The following year, in 1973, Gerald Church, a member of the Broward Area Transportation Committee, came to a commission meeting to present tentative plans for the widening of A1A to a four-lane highway. He also suggested that Sample Road could be extended, saying that the extension would definitely lead to a bridge across the intracoastal. This was an event which the residents did not wish to see. According to the map submitted, the bridge would be constructed at about the location of the Landmark condominium. Vice Mayor Stradella's prediction at the time, "I don't believe it will ever happen," proved to be correct.

No matter what other issues intervened, the subject of density continued to be everpresent. Another aspect of zoning and density was addressed by Resolution 135, which prohibited further building in Hillsboro Beach until a municipal sewer system was completed. In 1971 construction had been tabled until the issue was resolved. One large county bond issue was approved ($1.3 million in Hillsboro Beach) to pay for construction of lines which would run into the county's proposed master treatment plant. Although the county would own and operate the systems, all costs in the area would be assumed by the assessment districts. Construction of the major sewer line was scheduled to begin April 15, 1974. The town system would be pumped to the North Broward sewage treatment plant at Copans Road and Powerline Road.

The new regional plant was to be in operation by June 1974, but A1A was torn up for that entire summer, and the project was not completed until November.

By June 1976, 79 of the 94 existing properties in Hillsboro Beach had completed their sewer connections and codification of ordinances had been completed. The commission accepted the $11,369.52 bid from Triple R. Paving, Inc., for constructing concrete sidewalks and resurfacing asphalt areas at Town Hall.

Also in 1976, George Patterson, who had been the town's prosecutor, resigned and was replaced by Judge O'Brien. Engineer Strock's monthly retainer increased from $300 to $500. The additional $200 was to cover the monthly retainer to the electrical and plumbing inspectors.

Again, concern over beach trespassers came to the town council. Repeated problems with surfers plagued the Port de Mer Condominium. This particular area along the beach was--and is--a long-time favorite of surfers because of the exceptional wave conditions. Tenants at Port de Mer, however, had become very upset when surfers used the outdoor showers and pool without tenants' permission. The commissioners authorized a sign to be posted at the north end of town stating that it was illegal for anyone to trespass on the land owned by Port de Mer. Once the sign was posted, authorities could cite violators. Access can now be obtained only from the public beach.

In 1977 commissioners were surprised to learn that the town owned a small bridge leading to the Hillsboro Island House. When the bridge was built, it had been dedicated to Hillsboro with the intention of giving the community a permanent right-of-way between the building and the mainland. Only when the town was notified that the bridge had not been inspected in compliance with state law and was in need of repairs, did the commissioners learn of the town's ownership.

Town Engineer Arthur Strock informed the town that the cost of repair would be $3,200. In a display of cooperation, the Hillsboro Island House agreed to share the cost. The Board of Directors at the Island House agreed to paint the bridge, repave the approach and replace the shrubbery. The town was left with the responsibility of repairing only the understructure of the bridge. Richard J. Purrington's bid of $2,497 for repairing the understructure was accepted. The town still owns the permanent right-of-way.

The people of Hillsboro had been by-passed by the Broward County Transportation Authority since May 1974. Bus service along A1A was inaugurated then in response to many requests, including petitions from residents. Before that time, a Pompano Beach bus from the south ran only to the Hillsboro Inlet, and a bus through Deerfield Beach ran to the Intracoastal Waterway along East Hillsboro Boulevard. The new bus ran a daily route on a regular schedule, although there were no scheduled stops in Hillsboro. Would-be riders had to flag the driver. The service lasted only until December 11, 1977, when it was discontinued.

In 1978, recycling began in Hillsboro Beach. Mayor Clyde Shaffer urged all residents to save their newspapers and bring them to the nearest container so that they could be recycled. "Recycling has proven to be a great ecological and money-saving venture and I would like to see total cooperation from the citizens of Hillsboro Beach in saving their newspapers," said Shaffer.

In 1979, the town installed a gas tank for the use of police and town cars. Another significant circumstance that year was the appearance of lethal yellowing, a fatal disease attacking coconut palms. Many trees in the city were dying, and citizens requested the town's help in removing dead trees.

That year the town had 1,205 registered voters and 30 fire hydrants. The Hillsboro Club suffered a serious fire from lightning, reporting the damage at $700,000. Hillsboro's fire service was turned over to Deerfield Beach. The contract for one year cost Hillsboro $70,270. Fire service for the U.S. Coast Guard and the Lighthouse Station continued to be provided by Pompano.

Fifth Decade: The '80s

In June 1980 several Cuban refugees were picked up on the beach and promptly sent to customs in Miami. The town disposed of the boats at its own expense. Through the '80s and into the '90s, refugees fleeing famine and repression have continued to pour into the United States via South Florida. Many have died in the attempt. Hillsboro Beach has not been spared such despair. The worst recorded refugee disaster in South Florida took place on the beaches of Hillsboro.

At dawn on October 26, 1981, a 32-foot boat named *La Nativite* capsized, and the waves which washed over it threw its human cargo to shore. Strewn along a mile stretch of the beach in Hillsboro, 33 of *La Nativite*'s 63 passengers lay dead. It was a tragic ending to a two-month journey from Haiti, including a month's stay in Cuba. The powerful beacon of the lighthouse had very likely attracted the boat, as it had many others.

Chief of Police Ralph Dunn and other officers had the unpleasant detail of removing the bodies and dealing with the aftermath. The beach was declared a disaster area after a news helicopter nearly collided with a Coast Guard cutter. Two immigration buses took the survivors from the police station to the Krome Avenue Detention Center in Miami, about 70 miles away. The immigrants were later released to friends and relatives.

Neither the catastrophe of October 1981 nor many similar ones stopped the waves of refugees that washed ashore in Florida throughout the '80s. In 1980 alone, more than 100,000 Cubans entered Florida in the Mariel boatlift.

The space shuttle *Columbia* was launched from Cape Canaveral under the command of pilot John Young, a Florida native, in 1981. The year was eventful in Hillsboro Beach as well. A Hurricane Commission was named, with members George Rovin, Pamela Kendall, H. Waldron and M. Lubratovich. In other business, the city granted a 30-year franchise to FPL, approved the fire contract with Deerfield Beach for $97,356.26, and received sealed bids for an addition to Town Hall and the police station.

The '80s proved to be disastrous for citrus farmers. In 1983 a freeze devastated the industry, with 10 percent of citrus acreage lost. Other freezes hit the crops in 1985 and 1989.

In 1983 Mayor Grainger asked Congressman Shaw to explore the possibilities of having a post office substation in Hillsboro Beach. As it had in the past, the government denied the request. Not until July 13, 1995, was there some postal relief, when an official post office substation opened just south of the inlet bridge.

A look back at Hillsboro Beach in the '80s is provided by Jennifer L. Schenker's candid article, "Old

Guard--1995 Changes Face, But Not Character," which appeared in February 1982 in the Fort Lauderdale *Sun Sentinel*:

Just past A TOUCH OF CLASS DRYCLEANERS, over Hillsboro Inlet's bridge, seagulls swoop past black clumps of seaweed, oblivious to the banging of the hammers and the whizzing of the saws. They dip and dive for breadcrumbs thrown by a bluejeaned hardhat perched on the second floor ledge of an oceanfront home undergoing renovations.

Below, on the beach, a bikini-clad English lord is out for a walk with a lady, strolling past a pink and blue house and the remains of a wrecked sailing craft.

During World War II, Sir Winston Churchill and President Franklin D. Roosevelt stayed in the pastel home just passed. On Oct. 26, a battered boat and the bodies of 33 Haitians washed up on the sand they have been walking on.

Neither visit ruffled the calm of Hillsboro Beach more than briefly.

"Most of the time when the wind's not blowing you could probably hear a pin drop from one end of town to the other," [said] Ralph Dunn, who has the enviable job of running a police department that has never investigated a murder in the 18 years he has been there. His officers spend most of their time ticketing speeders on State Road A1A.

But Hillsboro Beach--a town with no stores, no gas stations, no stoplights, no schools, no churches, one road, and the oldest population in the county--is changing.

Slowly, concrete condos and co-ops are edging out the pigeon plum, wild olive and ficus trees that once lined State Road A1A from one end of town to the other.

Only 467 people lived there in 1960, only about 1,500 now. This year five more condominiums are going up in the 3.2-mile long town, which in most places is only 450 feet wide.

The new construction, which will add an estimated 500 to 600 new residents, makes one of Broward's smallest towns one of its fastest-growing.

"Percentage wise that's a big jump," said Bill Kelley, the town's part-time building official.

It's a jump that started gradually, in the 1950s, when a few small tourist motels were built.

The condos came in the early '70s and by 1979 the landmark Barefoot Mailman hotel began converting to a time-sharing resort. Both developments changed the face of the town, but not its character.

At The Barefoot Mailman, for example, the residents include a young heiress and her chauffeur and an English peer from the Isle of Man.

Then there's the truck driver. Somewhat abashed by his neighbors' affluence, he calls himself a "truckologist," said complex manager Drew Apgar.

The truckologist is a rarity. Most Hillsboroites have two things in common--age and tax bracket.

"If you live here, you don't need a job," Dunn said. Those who need jobs--Dunn and the rest of the town's 12-man police force included--can't afford to live in the town where they work.

It is a town where old money means just that. Figures from the 1980 census show Hillsboro Beach's population has the highest median age in the county--66.8 years.

Two private schools that once operated in the town--the Lake Placid School for Boys, the main building of which is now part of the private Hillsboro Club, and the Country Day School, which was bulldozed in 1963 to make way for a condominium--are no longer needed, said Mayor Jack Erickson. He said there are "no children" to speak of in the seaside town.

"The young ones are in their 60s," said police officer Gary Liccardi.

Hillsboro began turning into a repository for the rich soon after Nick and Laura Moseley bought the first home on what is known as "Millionaires' Mile" back in 1947.

As the sun bounced off the silvery guard rails on her ailing husband's bed one recent afternoon, Mrs. Moseley, 81, reminisced with her spouse about the Hillsboro of old.

Raccoons and foxes peeked from behind the sea grapes when the Moseleys and 10 other families who helped settle the town held the first commission meeting 35 years ago--a picnic lunch on an oceanside lawn.

"We were like-minded people who loved the simple life with all the luxurious attachments," she said.

Luxurious attachments are an integral part of the town's 56 private homes. One house--which a subcontractor estimates will be worth $2.5 million when renovations are completed---sports sauna, whirlpool, fireplace and bar, and that's just in the master bedroom.

On weekends A1A--Hillsboro's only road--is jammed with gawking motorists who slow down to see "how the other half lives," Chief Dunn said. Most come away with only a glimpse, since the homes are hidden by lush foliage along the highway and the entire beach is private--posted with "No Trespassing" signs.

In Hillsboro Beach, the "other half" includes former mayor Charlie Stradella, retired board chairman and president of General Motors Acceptance Corp.; well-known heart specialist Dr. Ted Carson; Frances Parker, widow of Kenneth Parker of Parker Pens; and Amway Products President Richard Devos.

"They get an awful lot of certified mail," said postman Robert Slack, 52, whose mail route runs from the historic lighthouse on the south end to the Opals Tower East Condominium on the north.

"Their way of life is to stay at home a lot," said Glen Frazer, 32, who runs Grill's Market in Deerfield Beach with family members. Groceries from his store are ordered by phone and delivered door to door. The shopping lists include prime cuts of meat and an occasional NATIONAL ENQUIRER, he said.

The names of Hillsboro residents are rarely spotted outside of society columns. Publicity and controversy are things to be shunned. Most are retired business people and can safely be labeled "conservative," said long-term town clerk Reba Blankenship. The town's records show most vote Republican, she said.

On the home front, things are equally quiet. "I see most of my neighbors in November and again in May but not in between," she said, adding that people who pay high prices for a view of both the Atlantic and the Intracoastal Waterway "come looking for peace and quiet."

Andre LaBonte shares the same view from the window of his co-op apartment, but some of his views differ sharply from other Hillsboroites. So does his lifestyle.

"You are looking at the youngest and least wealthy person in Hillsboro Beach," said LaBonte who is 30 to 40 years younger than most of his neighbors at the Hillsboro Windsor.

While most of his neighbors play golf or bridge, the 34 year old ocean engineer scuba dives for lobster on the reef.

He watches and worries as small motels are bulldozed to make way for new condominiums on the beach. "The dollar sign makes it all go," he said. "Soon this will be another Miami Beach."

* * *

In 1983 the county refused to grant building permits in the town without platting--the submission to the county of a legal detailed map of the property in conformance with the county's land-use plan. The county required that the town set aside 22.8 acres for parks--a figure arrived at by a mathematical formula--although town officials insisted there was no need for a park in Hillsboro Beach. County planners eventually agreed.

The county also desired to obtain an 80-foot right of way along two-lane A1A. None of the land in Hillsboro Beach had ever been platted, and all these provisions under the county's land-use plan were ardently opposed. A 1978 Broward County study, which was cited in the land-use plan, identified A1A as a possible four-lane highway.

Mayor Ann Grainger urged town residents to attend the public hearing held May 26, 1983, and offered transportation to those who needed it to get to the hearing and oppose the widening of A1A. Citizens responded overwhelmingly.

In 1982 the census in Broward stated that in the decade between 1970 and 1980, the population of Hillsboro Beach grew 32%--from 1,181 to 1,554 residents. Within that population 53% owned their own homes and 34% lived alone. While only 69 were 18 and younger, 878 were 65 and older; 66.8 was the median age. There were 29 homes worth more than $150,000. Of the 1,154 condominiums in town, only 6% were rented; monthly rent averaged $502.

In 1989 it was the opinion of the commission that the town should begin plans for a new police building. This did not occur, and plans were not again revived for town restoration until 1996.

Also in 1989, the town's zoning ordinance needed revision to comply with the Comprehensive Land Use Plan. A board was appointed: G. Milot, S. Satullo, P. Cianci, K. Pinkerton, B. Suflas, J. Shultz and F. DeGennaro.

In a 37-page report, state officials cited at least six instances in which Hillsboro Beach failed to comply with major state planning requirements. Among the concerns were public access to the beaches, failure to develop a hurricane evacuation plan, protection of environmentally sensitive lands and endangered species, and standards for water, sewer and recreation services.

In January of 1989, county planners had unveiled a list of 32 natural areas which they claimed deserved the ultimate protection--purchase by Broward taxpayers for perpetual preservation. A rare dune and coastal forest in Hillsboro Beach was included, mainly the Freidt-Kennerly tract of 10.5 acres.

Plans called for the county to build two nature centers. At the site in Hillsboro Beach, non-native Australian pine trees would be removed to make way for parking spaces. A boardwalk would be built to keep people off the native sea grapes and sea oats, as well as provide public access to the beach. Shortly after the plans were announced, outraged Hillsboro residents and county officials intervened when the owner began to bulldoze part of his property.

County officials had made plans and provisions for clearing the sites as well as operating them, hoping to seize the moment and acquire the property quickly. There was opposition, however, for town residents still opposed giving any public access within the boundaries of Hillsboro Beach.

Their desire to retain the privacy they had always enjoyed was not an easy position to defend. In 1987 the developer wanted to rezone the property to build a seven-story project to care for the elderly. The plan prompted homeowners to form the organization of the Hillsboro Beach Property Owners Association. The group gathered 600 signatures and forced the property owners to withdraw the rezoning request.

The struggle did not end there. The developer returned to discuss rezoning for a resort hotel. Residents opposed the hotel in part because it would include a restaurant with a liquor license.

Realizing that they would face a long series of battles over rezoning, the homeowners became favorable to the preservation of the natural habitat developed by the county.

On March 14, 1989, voters were asked whether they would approve the $75 million bond issue to buy environmentally sensitive lands. The question stated:

Shall bonds of Broward County in an aggregate principal amount not exceeding $75,000,000 be issued under NO. 89-285, with a maturity not exceeding 30 years from their date, as determined by the board of county commissioners, bearing interest at a rate not exceeding the legal rate, as determined at time of sale and payable from unlimited ad valoren taxes, to provide funds to acquire, preserve or otherwise enhance environmentally sensitive lands in Broward County?

Six months later the County Commission deleted the Hillsboro Beach site from the protected list in a 5-2 vote. County parks officials recommended abandoning the Hillsboro Beach property, saying the land, appraised at $12 million, was too expensive.

Town commissioners in 1989 performed double duty, serving as members of the Zoning Board of Appeals. That year Edith Lederberg, of the Area Agency on Aging of Broward County, spoke to the commission on "fair share." The agency received $1,968 for the town's share of services rendered to its seniors.

Sixth Decade: The '90s

In 1990 those appointed to the Citizens Erosion Committee were Jan Moran, Don Mahoney and F. Paul Kendall. The Zoning Board consisted of G. Milot, S. Satullo, P. Cianci, Betty Henn, M. Norman, I. Brinegar and J. Shultz. Maurice O. Rhinehardt was reappointed as Town Attorney.

Walter Keller continued his service for the town's Comprehensive Plan and Land Development Regulations. Attorney Rhinehardt resigned at the end of 1990 and was replaced by Ellen Mills Gibbs. David Denman was granted the contract as the new town clerk in January 1991.

In 1991, after numerous conflicts, the town passed a noise ordinance and a dog ordinance. The Interlocal Agreement with the county for inspection of building and other official services was also passed that year.

Building, taxes and services continued to be town issues. In April 1993 the Interlocal Agreement with Broward County was approved for transportation services, subject to a $10,000 subsidy by the city. Also in 1993, Deputy Clerk Darlene Pfister received a 15-year service plaque.

Commissioners, once again, suggested that Town Hall be extended. The plans room was very inconvenient, and the roof leaked. Commissioner Grainger suggested that the conference room be used and that the building be extended. A new roof was later completed on Town Hall, but there were no new renovations.

On July 28, 1994, Judy Wilson's article "A1A Widening Begins This Month; DOT Limiting Traffic to One Lane" appeared in *The Deerfield Beach Observer*, highlighting the biggest issue in Hillsboro at the time. It read:

> *Millions of dollars in tropical landscaping, planted to the edge of A1A, will be crunched beneath bulldozers this summer, victim of a construction project from SE 2 Street in Deerfield Beach to the Landmark Condominium in Hillsboro Beach.*
>
> *Florida DOT is constructing a paved, four-foot shoulder on each side of the road with $1.8 million in federal enhancement funds.*
>
> *During the two-month construction period, which was scheduled to begin this week, traffic will be squeezed into one lane between 9 A.M. and 4 P.M.*
>
> *Residents were notified last week that anything standing within eight feet of the road should be removed, which caused some consternation among property owners who had been prepared to sacrifice their shrubs, lighting and other amenities within four feet of the road.*

* * *

In 1989, Hillsboro Beach saw the development of another community group of a different nature: the Women's League. This organization's philosophy was defined as follows: "The Women's League of Hillsboro Beach shall be women working for charity. Through this charity work the women shall develop a sense of community."

The first president, Kathy Pinkerton, activated the organization with ten charter members. Since 1989, they have hosted many charitable events and raised nearly half a million dollars for such charities as the American Cancer Society, Hospice by the Sea, the Children's Home Society, Coral Springs Medical Center Juvenile Diabetes Camp and Joe DiMagio's Children's Hospital.

Today there are close to 60 homes along the Magnificent Mile. The population is still the oldest in the county, with an average age of 66.

Nearly everyone seems to be law-abiding. In 1995, Hillsboro Beach was voted as being the most crime-free town in South Florida. The lack of conflict in the town explains why City Clerk David Denman says there's hardly ever any good gossip floating around.

Tourism is thriving as never before all over Florida, and the state has seen huge capital investments. Florida has observed its 150th anniversary and approaches the year 2000 with great aspirations. Hillsboro Beach finds itself, as the 21st century approaches, a town whose citizens are proud of their community and confident of their future.

9

Founders and Pioneers

Ernest Wooler

Little did the 14 voters know on March 4, 1947, that they had elected a highly creative perfectionist as their first mayor. This 5'4" dynamo was immediately challenged with what he envisioned for this oceanside town.

Born on February 26, 1888, in Manchester, England, Ernest was the oldest of six children (five sons and one daughter) of Ann Elizabeth Kayley and Herbert Wooler. Ernest was called "Little Ernie" for many years as a child and later as a young man, to distinguish him from his close friend Ernest Hives.

Both men dated the Warwick girls, who lived in the rectory across the footbridge where they lived in Manchester. Hives married Gertrude Warwick. Years later, after Wooler had been in America for some time, he also married a girl named Gertrude.

After finishing his elementary education at St. Margaret's Elementary School, Ernest attended the Science School for a couple of terms. His father, in a quandary over what to do with his eldest son, desired that Ernest continue with his course of study and become an engineer like himself. The boy loved mathematics, mechanical drawing and all practical subjects. He took pride in his drawing skill, so much so that for years he kept a pencil drawing of a motorcycle, drawn in 1903 and exhibited at Owen's College.

Herbert, after consulting many of his friends about what course Ernest's education should take, brought them together in his front parlor to come to some conclusion on the matter. It was decided that Ernest should sit for the Owens College matriculation examination in all subjects. If he passed, he would then devote all his time to engineering and get his B.Sc. degree more quickly. An excerpt from Ernest's diary tells what happened;

> *I sat for the matric. exam and failed in English and French. I hated languages anyway. No matter! I then had a private tutor coach me especially in languages. One had to take at least two of 'em. I failed a second time, but only in English and the next Monday morning went to work in the drawing office of Royce Ltd., August 1903. I ran errands, made easy tracings, made blue prints and "visited," especially with the draughtsmen. Learned electrical terms, attended Manchester Municipal School of Technology three nights a week taking machine drawing, electrical calculation and other subjects pertaining to electrical engineering, my vocation at Royce Ltd.*
>
> *I occasionally had contact with the great Pa Royce of whom I was scared to death. He had been a visitor at our home on a few rare occasions, but Mr. Claremont and Mr. John DeLooze often visited with father. Still they were very important people, in my mind, being father's bosses.*
>
> *I had not been in the office very long, until one*

day I was called into Mr. Royce's office. There he stood. He bawled me out for scribbling on the drawing sketches on the draftman's drawings. I admitted my error and after a few minutes of a severe lecture, Pa Royce said "Get me a typist's notebook." I dashed off to the stock room and got a notebook. When I offered it to him he said "You keep that and come with me." I followed him in fear and trembling down the steps in the shop where he motioned to Ernie Mills, a red-headed fitter, who joined the procession out of the shop and across the street to a stable where he kept his little two-cycle Decauville car in which he drove to the works every day from Knutsford. I'd heard of this motor car but had never seen it before. He explained that he and Ernie Mills would dismantle it and I was to make sketches of the important parts in the notebook and put on the dimensions.

* * *

And so from those drawings, two experienced motor car engineers designed the two-cylinder Royce car. Ernest helped on the project and was a premium apprentice to electrical engineering. His indentures were later changed to motor car manufacture. The first chassis of this venture was shown at the Paris Salon in 1904. They were made by Royce Ltd at Cooke Street and sold exclusively by C.S. Ross and Co. in Mayfair.

In March 1906 Rolls-Royce Limited was registered. At that time the share capital belonged to Royce Ltd. or the directors. Later in 1906, shares were floated to meet the financial needs of launching "The Silver Ghost," moving to a new purpose-built factory in Derby and absorbing C.S. Rolls & Co.

In 1913 Ernest left England for America. His nephew, Ernest Roy Wooler, now living in Lancaster, recalls very little about Uncle Ernest, having met him on only two or three occasions. "At that time," he says, "the two large shipping lines, White Star and Cunnard, were engaged in a price war for control of the Atlantic crossing. I am told the price fell to only three pounds. Rolls Royce then ran a works trip there. Ernest went and stayed. Things after that became rather vague."

In 1913 Rolls Royce had a base in New York for car servicing, long before Rolls Royce of America, Inc., opened its factory in Springfield, Massachusetts, in 1921. Ernest may have been sent to study some aspect of automotive engineering. He visited America under the sponsorship of the British Institute of Automotive Engineers. He remained in America and became chief designer for the Continental Motor Co. of Muskegan, Michigan.

In 1915 Ernest moved to Cleveland, Ohio, and became chief engineer for the Chandler Motor Car Company. During World War I he was liaison engineer in the conversion of farm tractors to tanks. These tanks became the first British Military tanks.

At this time he married Gertrude Ingersoll and decided that it was time to become an American citizen.

In 1926 he became chief engineer of the Timkin Roller Bearing Company in Canton, Ohio, which covered the entire United States on automotive and industrial machinery. He visited national projects as consulting engineer and attended two International Engineering Conferences in Europe as the American delegate.

In 1938 Ernest became Chief Engineer of Bower Roller Bearing Company in Detroit. During the tremendous expansion of this company, he assisted Packard in building the Rolls Royce aircraft engine during World War II. He also worked on all kinds of war equipment, which culminated in visiting England at the request of the British Ministry of Aircraft Production on Rolls

Royce "Merlin" engines. The engine was used in the legendary "Spitfire" planes which saved England from Hitler's bombers.

Ernest had long anticipated retirement in Florida. It is not known when he first visited the area, but he did visit the Hillsboro Club in 1935, at that time purchasing his lot in Hillsboro Beach. In 1939 and '40 he built a home on the lot, and he retired immediately after the end of World War II, moving to his new home town.

Still full of energy, he began the organization of the town, was elected mayor and handled all offices for three years. He held a combination post of mayor-police chief-tax collector-tax assessor, since there were so few officials to assume the various duties. Ernest kept a daily diary of his duties in town and hand-wrote all the minutes of meetings. He became actively engaged in resolving the problem of beach erosion, seeing to water plant installations, and participating in all other municipal activities. He visited and attended meetings of local municipalities to establish the best for the town. His life was Hillsboro Beach.

Having been a lover of sketching, Ernest later became fascinated with doodling. Perhaps his most famous doodle was conceived as he sat in Washington at a Republican National convention, on the night when Herbert Hoover was nominated to run for President of the United States. As Ernest scribbled, he discovered the possibilities for making a caricature of himself from the letters of his name.

The letter W reminded Wooler of his chin. The two O's became his eyeglasses, the L his nose, the E his mustache, and the R his mouth. He wrote the letters of his first name so that they became the hairline and outline of his head in the caricature.

In the *Fort Lauderdale News*, Monday, November 27, 1961, there appeared an article titled, "He Doodled to a Life's Profession," by Barbara Adams. She wrote:

> *. . . People noticed Wooler's signature and it never failed to raise an eyebrow or two. The syndicated column* Believe It Or Not *by Ripley carried the caricature for all the world to chuckle about.*

As time went by the caricature-signature became Wooler's trademark. He now used it on letterheads, envelopes, and disk memos.

FACE SIGNATURE
... believe-it-or-not

Ernest's energy and perfectionism beyond belief was evident in all his undertakings. Besides his diaries, he kept logs of hurricanes, planted palm trees along A1A, drew diagrams and sketches to aid in preventing erosion on the beach.

During World War I he had become an advanced pilot and junior navigator with the Grosse Pointe Power Squadron. He later became Commander of the Fort Lauderdale Power Squadron in 1951-52 and taught piloting. Always very active in many civic affairs in Broward County, he helped organize and build St. Martin's Episcopal Church and Vicarage and acted as clerk of the works for the Pompano High and Blanche Ely Schools. He was also active in the St. Nicholas Episcopal Church in Pompano Beach, the Deerfield Country Club, and the Audubon Society.

His health failing, he entered Holy Cross Hospital in 1968, where he had surgery to correct the lack of circulation in his legs. He passed away on June 24, 1969, and was buried in the Highlands Cemetery in Highlands, North Carolina.

George Russell French
contributed by James M. French

George Russell French was the son of John H. French Sr., a Detroit manufacturer and capitalist. As an adult in his home town, Russell was a director and senior vice president of the French Mortgage and Bond Company. His wife, Frances Moran, was descended from a family which can be traced back to the earliest French settlers in Detroit. The Moran family original land grant came from the King of France in approximately 1705.

Russ and Frances moved to Hillsboro Beach in 1948, building one of the first houses on the Hillsboro Mile. He was mayor of Hillsboro Beach from 1952 to 1955.

An avid yachtsman, Russ spent approximately half the year going up the inland waterway to Grosse Pointe, Michigan, which was his family home. Yet he put down very firm roots in south Florida, farming a large acreage west of Hillsboro Beach, raising green beans for the northern market. He was also founder and first chairman of the First National Bank of Pompano. He moved to Pompano in the late 1960s.

Russ French died on June 13, 1977, in Pompano. He is buried in the family plot in Woodlawn, a Detroit cemetery. His only surviving child is Mrs. Larry Sampler, who, it is my understanding, acted as secretary of

Hillsboro Beach for a considerable period.

Russ was fun to be with. I remember him as a generous, kindly, family-oriented person, who was a favorite with everyone around him.

Edward Reilly Stettinius

One of the most well known political figures who vacationed in Hillsboro Beach was Edward Stettinius, who owned a home at 924 Hillsboro Mile.

Little is known about Edward's holidays in Hillsboro Beach, although some world-famous political leaders were his guests from time to time. Bink Glisson, who worked as a caretaker for the Stettinius estate, today recalls that President Franklin Roosevelt liked to come there to relax. Another war-time leader who visited the estate was Prime Minister Winston Churchill. Many conferences took place on the Hillsboro Beach estate during World War II, with participants Roosevelt and General George Marshall, among others.

Born in Chicago, Illinois, on October 22, 1900, Stettinius had attended the University of Virginia as a young man. In 1931 he became vice president of General Motors, and three years later moved to U.S. Steel, eventually becoming chairman of the company in 1938. In 1939 he served on the country's War Resources Board. Also on the Council of National Defense Advisory Commission, he spurred development of synthetic rubber and worked in the Office of Production Management as lend-lease administrator and undersecretary of state.

As U.S. Secretary of State (1944-45), Stettinius advised President Roosevelt at Yalta and helped draw up the Act of Chapultepec in Mexico City.

After heading the U.S. delegation to the U.N. Charter Conference, he resigned to become his country's first permanent representative to the U.N. He left in 1946 and was elected rector of the University of Virginia.

He died in Greenwich, Connecticut, on October 31, 1949.

* * *

Alex D. Henderson

When Alex D. Henderson moved to Florida in 1946, he intended to retire. Instead, he founded the Hillsboro Country Day School. Located at the north end of Hillsboro Beach--1238 Hillsboro Mile--the school opened in 1953 and quickly grew to 150 students and 11 teachers. Henderson, far from retiring, was an active administrator.

The school's purpose was to prepare youngsters for acceptance to the best preparatory schools. The curriculum, from nursery through eighth grade, was designed with that in mind.

Alex had been associated with Avon products for 27 years, and he remained on its board of directors. It was the dividends from his stock in the Avon Company that enabled him to pursue his philanthropy--and his wife's, after his death.

"A.D.," as he was called, "believed that all children could be successful and it was up to the teacher to make it happen," recalls Barbara Bittner, a former teacher at the school. His commitment to children, parents and teachers was shown in a school calendar punctuated with family events: catered dinner parties for parents, Halloween and Christmas events, and a spring fair that was the highlight of the school year. He built what was then the largest privately owned swimming pool east of the Mississippi and set the standard that all students would know how to swim by the end of their first year of attendance.

A separate program for winter visitors was established. The first principal of HCDS lived at the school.

Enrollment grew to 300, with students drawn from surrounding towns from as far away as Royal Palm and Lauderdale-by-the-Sea.

The first two teachers--Norma Cope and Lorraine Harry--lived in Pompano. Every year at Christmas, each teacher at HCDS received 25 shares of the Avon Company.

After A.D.'s death in 1964, the school was moved to the Florida Atlantic University campus. His widow, Lucy Henderson Edmondson, was the benefactor, making the bequest in memory of her late husband. The Alexander D. Henderson University School opened in 1968. Located on 23 acres on the FAU campus in Boca Raton, Florida, the school's logo depicting the Hillsboro Lighthouse serves as a reminder of A.D.'s leadership and the school's beginning as a private school, the Hillsboro Country Day School. Today it is an endowed public school. Admission is by lottery, and 450 students are in attendance.

Barbara Bittner, who served as the school's principal/director for more than 25 years, recalls that A.D. was a very generous man. When Alex saw a need, he took care of it.

Henderson was a significant contributor to St. Andrew's School and donated the land for the Henderson Clinic in Fort Lauderdale. He became active in Hillsboro Beach politics and was acting mayor from 1958 until he died, in 1964.

Arthur "Bink" Glisson

A native Floridian, Bink was born on August 2, 1914, in Weleka, Florida (located on the St. John's River). Lured by the sea, Bink became a fisherman and later enlisted in the U.S. Navy. He has many memories of all the action which he saw during World War II.

In 1942 while stationed in Key West, he was introduced to Edward Stettinius by Captain E.T. Knight (Bink's uncle), the owner of Cap's Place. (Two years later, Stettinius became secretary of state under President Roosevelt.) The introduction led to a long-lasting friendship between Glisson and Stettinius and many fishing trips together.

Bink eventually became the caretaker for the property of Stettinius at 925 Hillsboro Mile. There he got first hand glimpses of the illustrious political leaders who visited his distinguished employer. In 1949 after Edward's death, Bink stayed on to help Mrs. Stettinius sell the property to C. Oliver Wellington, from Boston.

After the sale, Bink stayed on to work for the Wellingtons. They subsequently gave him the responsibility of finding property in which to invest. He zeroed in on the land now known as A.I.D. (Acme Improvement District). Today this estate is known as Wellington, located in Palm Beach County.

Most of Bink's life has been dedicated to community service. He was one of the original Hillsboro Inlet District Commissioners. Besides being in the U.S. Navy, he has been a pilot, boat captain, naturalist and artist. At present, he is working to create an historical museum. A friend of the Seminoles, his interests are in preserving for the future.

After the death of his first wife, Genevieve Campbell, he married Joan Sawyer, who is also dedicated to the community. Together they are working to establish their museum, called the Memory Barn.

Floyd Grainger

Born in Tampa, Floyd Grainger moved back to his native state from Atlanta, Georgia in 1958. He and his wife, Ann, and their daughter, Ann, settled in

Hillsboro Beach.

Everyone knew each other in Hillsboro Beach in the '50s. There were no high rise condominiums and only a few low rise co-ops and motels, which were located on the north end of town. Also located at the north end of town was the Hillsboro Country Day School founded by Alex Henderson.

Young Ann loved the school and attended through sixth grade.

Floyd was a Georgia Tech graduate and a real estate developer. He had built many single family homes and apartments in the Atlanta-Austell, Georgia, area before coming south. After he moved to Hillsboro Beach he continued working as a developer. Among his accomplishments was the development of Tiara East in Deerfield Beach. One of his first projects was the condominium conversion of Royal Palm Villas.

Grainger was very community oriented, and he became director and first vice president of the Deerfield Beach Chamber of Commerce. In 1964 he was appointed to the Town Commission of Hillsboro Beach and after the death of Mayor Alexander D. Henderson, became mayor in 1965.

Floyd and wife Ann established the Westminister Foundation, Inc., which established non-profit housing for 475 elderly in Delray Beach. Today this development is called the Lake Delray Apartments.

At the age of 50, Floyd lost his battle with cancer; he passed away in 1979.

Charles Gillet Stradella
From the *Fort Lauderdale Sun-Sentinel*, June 21, 1989
written by Kevin Allen

Automotive industry pioneer Charles Gillet

Stradella, who retired to Hillsboro Beach and served as its mayor and town commissioner, died at home on Monday. He was 91.

Mr. Stradella was a member of the board of directors at General Motors Corp. when he retired in 1962 after 42 years with the company.

He also was chief executive officer of the company's financing arm, General Motors Acceptance Corp., which he joined eight months after the subsidiary was organized in 1919.

"He was there from the very beginning of GMAC," said John Zimmerman, who succeeded Stradella as head of the company. "He was a delight to work for, absolutely fair. GMAC is people and money, and that's what he was best at."

Mr. Stradella also was instrumental in launching GMAC's European operation, serving in a variety of executive positions before and after World War II.

He was named head of GMAC and was a member of the GM board of directors in 1954.

"He always said the friends that he made were the most important thing to him," said his wife, Marilyn. "That's really what meant the most to him. He was always a contributor to whatever town he lived in."

Mr. Stradella was born in North Tonowanda, New York, and graduated from Yale University in 1919. While working at General Motors, he attended Fordham Law School and was admitted to the New York State Bar in 1924.

He spent winters in Florida before retiring, and built a winter home in Hillsboro Beach in 1937. It was the town's first single-family home, said town clerk Reba Blankenship.

Mr. Stradella moved to Hillsboro Beach permanently in 1962, and four years later was elected to the town commission. He served as mayor from 1969 to 1970 and vice mayor from 1972 to 1973.

He was instrumental in passing two large municipal bond issues, one for a beach renourishment project and another for additions to the town's water system.

"He was a financial genius," Blankenship said. "He was one of the best I've ever seen at it. When he went off the commission we had quite a budget surplus."

In 1988, he was appointed to a board to monitor beach erosion.

Mr. Stradella remained interested in town affairs, attending commission meetings regularly until six months ago.

He also served on the boards of many business and civic organizations, including the New York Lighthouse for the Blind, Holy Cross Hospital in Fort Lauderdale and First Union Bank of Pompano Beach.

He is survived by his wife, Marilyn; a son, Charles Jr., of Fort Lee, New Jersey; a daughter, Marjorie Hodgman of Cornwall, Connecticut; two grandchildren and two great grandchildren.

Keith MacKenzie Brooks
contributed by Dennis K. Brooks

"He was a friendly man." My father wrote this about himself in his high school year book in 1928; he remained a friendly man all the years of his life.

He was born in Rivers, Manitoba, on January 10, 1909, to Frank Brooks and Kathleen Elizabeth MacKenzie, and was the older brother of Kathleen Elizabeth Brooks (Anderson) and Seddon Bruce Brooks. He grew up in Rivers and Winnipeg, Manitoba, and Toronto and Sarnia, Ontario, and spent summers in Algonac, Michigan, where he learned to hun and fish.

When he was 14, he cut the tendon in his left index finger while working with a saw. There is a picture of him and his Aunt Bess, he with his left hand in a cast. Although the finger healed, it was permanently curled over, and he could not straighten it out for the rest of his life. It never bothered him and did not prohibit his entry into the U.S. Army in World War II or getting a job selling men's gloves for the J.L. Hudson Company in Detroit. His grandchildren actually found it very convenient to hold onto this particular finger when walking with their granddad.

The family moved to Detroit around 1925, and Keith graduated from Detroit Western High School in 1928. He attended college for one year at either Wayne State University or the University of Detroit and began work in the mortgage business in Detroit.

He married Dorothea "Dode" Louise Kittridege, after knowing her for three weeks, on March 23, 1937. He must have been doing all right, for they built a house on Robson Avenue in Detroit in 1938, and photos from the period indicate that they were successful. Keith and Dode--he called her "Chicken"--took summer vacations to Michigan Lakes with their neighbors Stan and Verne Burbridge. This became a yearly tradition that continued into the 1950s.

Keith enlisted in the U.S. Army on November 7, 1942, and underwent training at Fort Sill, Oklahoma. He was commissioned a 2nd Lieutenant and served as the Battalion Motor Officer for the 355th Artillery Battalion of the 76th Infantry Division in the 3rd Army under General George Patton. He saw action in France, Belgium and Germany and returned to the United States on August 25, 1945. He was awarded the Bronze Star for his service. A unique footnote to his service is the fact that he landed in

England on the day his son was born, December 21, 1944.

Re-entering the business world, Keith worked for Acme Home Builders until starting his own home-building/real estate business in 1952. He began by building and selling 28 middle class homes on Hanes Avenue in Birmingham, Michigan. Realizing that there was more money to be made in the upper end of the market, he started building custom homes in Birmingham and Bloomfield Hills, Michigan, around 1954. He was very successful, establishing an excellent reputation and continuing to build homes until he retired in 1968. He built about 10-12 houses a year. One of these was purchased by the Red Wings hockey star Gordie Howe. Most of Keith's houses were bought by auto industry executives. He sold his company in 1968, and he and Dode moved to Hillsboro Beach, Florida.

Keith's fascination and love of boats was one reason they retired to Hillsboro Beach. It was the only spot on Florida's East Coast that afforded an unobstructed view of both the ocean and the Intracoastal Waterway. They could see either view from their third floor apartment on A1A. Their living room fronted on the ocean and their bedroom on the Intracoastal Waterway. Keith's favorite view was of the boats on the waterway, and he could almost always be found spending happy hour in a chair watching the waterway traffic.

When he retired in 1968, Keith's only wish was for three good years of retirement; he got five and a half. He truly enjoyed living in Hillsboro Beach. He would walk the beach from their place to the Hillsboro Beach Lighthouse, one mile, daily. He and Dode also played golf and took golfing trips to the Bahamas. He volunteered his services to the town and re-wrote the town's zoning ordinances to restrict the further construction of high rise hotels and condominiums. In 1970 he was elected to the board of commissioners, and in 1972 he was elected mayor. In that role, he diligently worked to provide the town with an internal police force and external support of other required services from the neighboring municipalities. He was well known and well liked by all the citizens.

In 1973 Keith's platform for election stated:

> *I believe that most of us settled in Hillsboro Beach because of what we saw and liked. A friendly, quiet, uncrowded place, beautiful beach, a spot of lush green foliage nestled amid the sea of concrete that makes up a good part of the Florida southeast gold coast today. A spot where we could just relax and enjoy the sun and surf.*
>
> *During my past three years on the commission, my efforts have been directed at saving these amenities for all the citizens of the town, and if re-elected, I pledge to continue on this same course of action for the next two years.*
>
> *The top priorities now facing the town are the installation of a sewerage collection system and continued maintenance of the North Beach. I favor resolving both these matters as soon as possible. I also favor maintaining a full complement of competent police officers to enable our citizens to receive instant police protection when they request it.*
>
> *Your support of my re-election to the commission on March 6, 1973, will be appreciated.*

He was re-elected but died in office on July 10, 1973.

While Keith was active in politics, Dorothea was very active in the North Broward Hospital Auxiliary. She worked in the gift shop and as a buyer from 1968-1990, volunteering over 14,000 hours of service to the auxiliary. She remained in Hillsboro Beach until 1990 and passed away on August 4, 1996. The North Broward Auxiliary has established a memorial scholarship in her memory.

Clyde H. Shaffer

Clyde H. Shaffer was born in Hooversville, Pennsylvania, in January 1900. Two years later his father died. His mother married a minister/school principal, and the family lived in a number of small towns in western Pennsylvania.

In 1918 Shaffer joined the U.S. Army and was discharged a year later. He worked odd jobs for two years until he earned enough to attend Pennsylvania State University. There he pledged Sigma Alpha Epsilon, where he met Henry Breyer Jr.; they became fraternity brothers and lifelong friends.

Clyde would spend vacations at the Breyer estate in Pennsylvania--now the Cheltenham Township building. After Shaffer's graduation in 1925, Breyer's father, founder of the ice cream company, offered him a job as a trainee. Clyde had to work Sundays, but he loved the ice cream. He was a very thin man and claimed the ice cream kept him alive.

He moved progressively up the executive ladder at the company, serving as office manager, then manager of the New York City plant, vice president for Philadelphia, and then New York operations and treasurer before becoming president of the company in 1941, a position he held until 1965.

During the Kennedy administration, Jacqueline Kennedy's secretary called Shaffer requesting a small amount of Pistachio ice cream for a party. Because flavors were seasonal, Clyde couldn't make just a few gallons, so he made 50 gallons and gave the remainder--after filling the Kennedy order--to his employees.

The company bought in such volume that when it

purchased ingredients for butter pecan, it so depleted the supply of pecans that prices for available nuts would soar.

At home, the Shaffers had a freezer like one found in a drugstore.

Clyde served on the board of directors of National Dairy Products Corporation (which bought out Breyers in 1929) and later on the board of the Kraft Corporation (which acquired the company in 1952). At one time he was also president of the International Milk and Ice Cream Association.

In 1965 Clyde retired and came to Florida with his wife, née Elizabeth C. Smith, daughter of former Philadelphia Mayor Thomas B. Smith. They rented their first home in Pompano Beach, but eventually bought a home in Hillsboro Beach and moved here permanently.

Clyde was not content to sit around. He looked up the zoning regulations in neighboring towns in order to improve the existing zoning in Hillsboro Beach. He was eventually put in charge of the zoning and, as a result, was nicknamed "Five-story Shaffer."

A devoted resident and admirer of the police department, Clyde saw to it that they had equipment such as bullet-proof vests and badges. One of his favorite pastimes was to walk and clean the beach while meeting and talking with town residents.

Nearly 90 when he passed away, he had always been devoted to and admired by the community. He had been commissioner in 1972 and vice mayor in 1973. When he ran for office again in 1974, 55 percent of the electorate voted for him.

His widow, Elizabeth, today lives in Blue Bell, Pennsylvania.

John W. Erickson

contributed by Jacqueline L. Erickson

John W. Erickson was born in Chicago in 1902. The bulk of his working career was spent with Chocolate Products Company, manufacturers of chocolate and other flavorings for the dairy industry. Its products were distributed mainly in the midwestern states. He was executive vice president in charge of sales for 30 years until his retirement.

Jack, as he was called by everyone who knew him, came to Hillsboro Beach in the spring of 1967. He and my mother, LeMerle, arrived in Florida from Chicago, where they had been born and had spent all of their lives. They were looking for a retirement home in a quiet community and, after driving from Miami north to Palm Beach, ultimately settled on an apartment at the Hillsboro Windsor here in Hillsboro Beach.

Spending his golden years walking the beach and playing bridge as his only interests did not particularly appeal to my father. He became active in the cooperative community at the Windsor and did his stint as a board member, as do most people who retire to condominium life. He was drawn to the work on beach erosion as he saw, on his daily treks from the Deerfield Beach pier to the lighthouse, the sands washing out to sea and the sea walls of various condominiums and motels exposed to the pounding of the surf. He volunteered to work on the beach erosion committee of our town.

This led to his running for a seat on the commission in 1970--a seat he held until 1982, when he retired from public life as Florida's oldest mayor still active in municipal government, according to an account in the *Fort Lauderdale Sun Sentinel*.

In the mid-1970s, Jack Erickson was instrumental in obtaining the funds to dredge sand along Hillsboro Beach's three-mile coastline. He tried for federal funding first, but since we are a beach with no public access, that funding was denied. Ultimately the town put out a bond issue to pay for the replenishment of the sand. Residents of Hillsboro Beach who were here when the dredging took place can remember the abundance of shells coming ashore with the thousands upon thousands of cubic yards of sand dredged from a mile out to sea.

My father and I used to reminisce, often speaking of the work he did for our town--the work of which he was most proud. In addition to his work on beach erosion, he was pleased with a study of employee salaries at the town hall. He compared the salaries being paid at Hillsboro Beach with neighboring island communities--Highland Beach and Manalapan. Jack Erickson discovered our town was well below scale, and consequently everyone ended up getting a raise in pay.

Another of my father's major undertakings was the editing of the code of the town of Hillsboro Beach. Adopted in 1976, the compilation constituted a complete codification of the ordinances of our town. He also oversaw the renovation of the town hall just before his retirement in 1982.

"The town gave me the chance for an entirely new and different second career," my father said over and over. "Had I known public service could have been so rewarding and provide such personal satisfaction, I would have entered the public arena earlier in my life. I feel lucky to have found such a wonderful opportunity, not only to serve the people of our town but also to derive such a large measure of personal gratification."

And the job was an easy commute, too.

When my father served as commissioner and mayor, at various times during his dozen years in town service, the commissioners did not receive any pay for most of his terms of office. Just prior to his retirement, the commissioners put to a vote the instigation of a modest pay for themselves of $100 per month. Jack Erickson voted nay. "A job that is this much fun," he said, "doesn't require any monetary remuneration."

He died in Florida in 1987 and was survived by his wife, LeMerle (who would follow him in death in 1989), and by three daughters, the eldest of whom lives, as her parents did, at the Hillsboro Windsor here in Hillsboro Beach.

Ann Grainger

Born in Cartersville, Georgia, Ann Grainger attended the University of Georgia and graduated from Atlanta Law School. She is still, today, a member of the Georgia State Bar.

Ann met Floyd Grainger (who became mayor of Hillsboro Beach in 1965) when she worked in the Georgia attorney general's office. She was the closing attorney for a deal in which Floyd was involved.

After the couple and their daughter, Ann, moved to Hillsboro Beach in 1958, she, as well as her husband, shared the concerns of their new community. In 1981, because of her interest in Hillsboro Beach, she was asked by Jack Erickson to become a member of the commission. She served the town as commissioner in 1981-82, became mayor in 1983-87, commissioner again in 1988, mayor in 1989-90 and again commissioner in 1991-93.

Ann worked throughout the years with her husband in the development of real estate. She became a licensed realtor in 1979. During her term as mayor, the fluoride system was introduced to Hillsboro's water. She was a strong opponent of the widening of A1A and of the proposed park in the center of town which was intended for public use. She also encouraged the renovation of town hall and the commission room in 1983-84.

She continues to work in real estate. In 1993, Lou Godek, a prominent realtor who had dealt with many oceanfront properties, walked into her office and said, "Ann, I'm retiring." Ann asked him if she could think about buying his business and if she could consider it overnight. She did buy the business, and today works there with her daughter.

Edmund C. Jones

Edmund C. Jones lived in Hillsboro Beach for 21 years. He served on the town council in 1987 when he was appointed to complete the term of H. Spielman; in 1988 Jones served as mayor.

Born in Carbondale, Pennsylvania, he came here from Mountainside, New Jersey. Having started his working career in 1928 as an office boy with the Singer Sewing Machine Company in Philadelphia, he moved with subsequent promotions to Buffalo, Pittsburgh, Minneapolis and New York City. After 42 years with the company, he retired, having served as regional sales manager and director of human resources at Singer.

During World War II he had served in the U.S. Marine Corps at the Philadelphia Naval Yard. In the 1950s he served several terms as commissioner of Upper Saint Clair Township, outside Pittsburgh, and he continued his community service in Hillsboro Beach when he retired. Edmund also served on the board of directors of the Deerfield Country Club and Opal Towers, where he resided.

He passed away on September 19, 1994, at the age of 86.

Erwin H. Haass
from *The Detroit News*, June 12, 1994
written by J.R. Clairborne

Services for Erwin H. Haass, an attorney, philanthropist and retired businessman, will be held at noon Wednesday in Christ Church, 61 Grosse Pointe Boulevard, Grosse Pointe Farms.

Mr. Haass, 90, formerly of Grosse Pointe Farms, died from an aneurysm Friday, June 10, 1994, in Bon Secours Hospital.

"To the very end, he was assisting the physician in any way he could to help the doctor help him," said son Frederick Haass. "He was that type of person."

Mr. Haass fell ill at his office at the Detroit law firm of Dickinson, Wright, Moon, VanDusen and Freeman, where he remained a consulting partner.

Mr. Haass, who was graduated from the University of Michigan, began his legal career with the Detroit firm of Race, Haass and Allen.

He was president and chairman of the Winter Haven Corporation of Winter Haven, Florida. He also headed the Erwin and Virginia Haass Foundation, which provides financial assistance to charities--especially churches and the Evangelical Homes of Michigan, his son said.

Mr. Haass served as president and director of the Goebel Brewing Company, which is now owned by Stroh's Brewing Company. He was also the director of City National Bank of Detroit and First National Bank, Pompano Beach, Florida.

He served in the U.S. Army Corps during World War II.

Survivors include his sons, Frederick E., Robert O., and Stephen A.; two daughters, Susan Klonowski and Sandra H. Haller and three grandchildren.

Entombment will be in Woodlawn Cemetery, Detroit.

Erwin was also a director of several corporations including the First National Bank of Pompano Beach. He was also a member of various clubs and organizations including the Hundred Club of Broward County and Royal Palm Yacht and Country Club in Boca Raton.

Herbert Whiting
contributed by Jacki O'Hara

Herbert Whiting was born in Buffalo, New York, in 1883, the son of a hat maker. After graduating from high school he went to work in sales for Jewitt Stove Company. In 1909 he was employed by Buffalo Forge Company, where he remained until his retirement, around 1958. He began as an office boy and gradually moved up, working as traffic manager, credit manager and office manager. He retired as vice president/secretary.

In 1907 Bert, as his friends called him, married Della Weller. Ten years later their only child, Virginia, was born. She was the apple of his eye throughout the many decades of his life.

In 1953, not long before Bert retired, he came to Hillsboro Beach to visit his daughter and her family, who were renting a villa at The Recess. It was obvious that not only did she and her family love the area and the beach here, but so did he. When told that the villa was to be sold and the family could not rent again the following year, Bert decided to buy it as his retirement home, a place which his family would enjoy visiting. Thus began what is now close to 45 years of family vacations here in Hillsboro Beach, a spot which his granddaughters, great grandchildren and great-great grandchildren are now able to enjoy.

The eight Recess villas were built in 1948 and were originally owned by six families as a cooperative. Those families included: Mr. and Mrs. Fred Berens of Washington, D.C.; Mr. and Mrs. C. Merill Beemis of Richmond, Virginia; Mr. and Mrs. Charles Davis of Detroit, Michigan; Mr. and Mrs. Howard S. Gier of Warren, Ohio; Mr. and Mrs. Art Schuman of Philadelphia, Pennsylvania; and Mr. and Mrs. Stanton Smith of Rockford, Illinois. The remaining two villas were purchased by Mr. and Mrs. Allen Long of Petersburg, Virginia, and Mr. Whiting.

During the mid-1950s, his granddaughters remember, they fished with their grandfather in the intracoastal on what is currently owned by Hillsboro Beach, the land on which the Town Hall and the Police Department are located.

In those early years, the owners of The Recess held title to the land on both sides of A1A. Trying to get to the intracoastal from the west side of the road was quite difficult, since the land on both sides of the waterway was virtually untouched by development at that time. The beach was very deep, perhaps sixty yards at low tide.

Not long after retiring to Hillsboro Beach, Bert Whiting bought a 21-foot clapboard Lyman boat which he docked at a very small marina just off US1 at the southern edge of Boca Raton. At that time, most of the intracoastal property remained undeveloped. He enjoyed taking his family for rides on the intracoastal, seeing and commenting upon the beginnings of property development taking place.

He and his family also enjoyed going to the Pancake House that was just south of the bend on A1A in Deerfield Beach. Waiting in line for one of the few tables was nothing unusual, but no one ever left hungry. Often Bert and his family would walk to the establishment and back, just to feel more comfortable after stuffing their tummies.

Walks on the beach were routine for the Whitings, and all of them became interested in shelling. A much wider variety and supply of shells were available during the 1950s that there are today. A walk north to the pier or south to the lighthouse was very enjoyable along the beach, which was very deep along the entire stretch of land. We often stopped at what we called "the Monkey House," a private home about a half mile north of The Recess, to view the owner's pet monkey.

In the 1950s Bert drove a Dodge two-door sedan, which, he decided, needed to be painted for rust protection from the salt air. What a surprise it was for his neighbors and family when the car returned a bright shade of orange. Bert was determined to have the auto rust-proofed, and that was the only color choice for the most protective paint. From then on, the car was known as The Orange Blossom Special.

Bert was an avid sports enthusiast. He was especially interested in the Triple A Buffalo Bisons and served as secretary of the baseball club, attending many of their games. It is with fond memories that this granddaughter remembers watching some of those games with him from the press box and following him into the locker room afterwards on more than one occasion. After his retirement to Hillsboro Beach, he enthusiastically followed the Bisons throughout their spring training during the several seasons it was held in Pompano Beach.

Bert was an avid gardener and specialized in growing roses. His garden, while he resided at The Recess, contained more than 50 bushes, and everyone around became a recipient of his bouquets. He delighted in giving them away and often took them to the town hall office. He maintained his garden until just two months before his death, and I truly believe that the joy he received from growing and giving away his flowers was what kept him vital and active.

He frequently attended auctions at the Deerfield Beach auction house, and several of his purchases remain in the family's villa. He was a member of the Deerfield Country Club and lunched there twice a week for more than two decades. On the occasion of his 100th birthday, his daughter hosted a party at the club and Bert was extended a lifetime membership.

In addition, Bert was a member of the First United Presbyterian Church of Deerfield Beach when Dr. Briggs was pastor. The Whitings attended the services there regularly. Bert and his family were part of the handful of people attending the first Easter Sunrise Service near the Deerfield Beach pier. It was held in a small pavilion then; only a dozen people were present.

Since Bert's death in 1984, which was one month shy of his 101st birthday, The Recess villa has remained in the family and is currently owned by his two granddaughters. Bert Whiting was a gentle man, a man who always cared for and about others, a man who lived his entire life without saying anything unkind about anyone. He was a wonderful father and grandfather and was grateful for everything he had. It is a privilege to have known him so well.

* * *

Howard "Chuck" Sussman

Elected commissioner in 1989, Chuck Sussman became mayor in 1993 and continues to serve his town.

Born in Bronx, New York, Chuck grew up in Cedarhurst and attended Adelphi College. In 1952 he enlisted in the U.S. Army and the following year married Greta Holzman. He held various command positions and served at Fort Knox, Kentucky, after graduating from Infantry OCS; he was discharged in 1955.

In his marriage of more than 40 years, Chuck has moved his family at least 15 times to keep abreast of the opportunities life constantly offered him. He has had great success as a salesman, but another side of him is his ability as an inventor. His creativity has led him to secure 36 U.S. patents, some on products which he designed, manufactured and sold himself.

He started his own companies along the way. A new company, Pretty Neat Industries, started in 1976, growing to be the largest manufacturer of cosmetic organizers in the world. In 1983 he moved the company to Pompano Beach and employed approximately 160 people. The company was selected for the prestigious "INC 500," a list of the 500 fastest growing, privately held companies in the country. The company was selected for the honor three times. Sussman sold the company in 1985, took it back six months later, engineered a turn around, and sold the company again in 1987.

Business does not completely fill his time, for he is community- and family-oriented. After moving his family to Hillsboro Beach in 1981, Chuck became involved in the town's politics--and he continues to be so. Avid motorcyclists, he and Greta travel many miles on Chuck's Harley each year. A big part of their lives is centered around their three children and their families. Chuck and Greta's oceanfront home is designed for the enjoyment of their six grandchildren.

Their world travels have taken them to the jungles of Central America and, on the Orient Express, from Bejing to Siberia. On their most recent trip, a cross country tour of the United States, they covered more than 12,000 miles with the Harley and their 1957 T-Bird.

10

The Police Department

The Town Marshal: Amo Angeletti

On November 9, 1948, the town commission approved the hiring of a town marshal. His salary was set at $150 per month, with his home and utilities being furnished by the town. He would serve as sheriff, fireman, watchman and waterman (handling meters and bills); he was to clean the roads and the beach, keep the town's books and dispense town information; and he would be in charge of fishing permits and similar licenses.

In January 1949, Hillsboro Mayor Ernest Wooler was attending the air show in Pompano Beach when he approached Amo Angeletti, a policeman on the Pompano Beach police force. Angeletti, married and the father of twin boys born in 1945, was subsequently hired as the first town marshal.

Amo, now a resident of Pembroke Pines, recalls all the residents of Hillsboro at that time and the common reference to Hillsboro Beach in those days as "Rattlesnake Ridge." He declares that in the town he met "some of the world's finest people." Remembering Ernest Wooler,

Angeletti describes him as "the typical Englishman, very devoted to Hillsboro Beach and very selfish of the town."

It was a community of "great people," and the town's first marshal considered them to be part of his family. Indeed, his youngest son, Danny, born in 1949, had the distinction of being the first child born in Hillsboro Beach after it was chartered.

As homes began to develop--the south and middle miles owned by Burwell Smith, owner of coal mines from Pennsylvania--lots were for sale for approximately $8300. Only one home at that time had a rope across the driveway; there were no gates. Patrolling the community, Amo would drive through each property. Turtle hunters were a constant nuisance, and the Blue Fish Hole was a very popular place for fishermen.

One of Amo's favorite stories is about the pants burglar, who struck homes from Palm Beach to Miami. Hillsboro Beach was no exception. Some of the victims lived at the north end of town, in one or another of the eight cottages Marie McCollom owned. At that time, people did not lock their houses; the burglar would simply walk in when he could do so unobserved. He would snatch men's trousers and women's pocketbooks, take them outside and shake them till they gave up their money and other valuables. Angeletti, happy to cooperate with all the police chiefs along the coast, was the law enforcement officer who eventually apprehended the burglar.

Weather was quite cool in January and February in those days. Amo recalls that frosts were common and warm clothing was needed. Also, a surge of mosquitoes required almost constant fogging.

Early one morning in 1949, Amo discovered large bundles of mahogany on the beach near the Blue Fish Hole. The storm during the night had caused a shipwreck nearby, and the spoils had reached the beach. The days of freedom to scavenge were long past, however, and a lawsuit ensued when the mahogany was claimed by two different residents.

Angeletti, who was responsible for designing the Hillsboro Beach logo, established the numbers on all residences and many artifacts that still exist today, such as the small lighthouse on the roof of today's town hall.

In 1951 and 1952 extra police were hired. The added stress culminated in circumstances which led to some unfortunate events, including five drownings. Because of his involvement as town marshal, Amo resigned from his position.

Angeletti had begun his career in the U.S. military service as a 1st sergeant in the Military Police. Then came his stint on the Pompano Beach police force and his job as town marshal of Hillsboro Beach. He went on to school in Philadelphia and became an electrical engineer, designing for various companies, among them DuPont, Monsanto, IBM, and Pratt & Whitney. Having retired in 1994, Amo is writing a book about the pants burglar.

The First Patrolman: Charles V. Kanode Jr.

"Chuck" Kanode was born in Lakeland, Florida. He attended Lakeland High School, then transferred to the Lodwick School of Aeronautics in Lakeland to become a flight line instructor. He was too young for the U.S. armed services during World War II, but as a flight line instructor he could still serve his country by training British cadets. He later attended Polk School of Business, completed a course in business administration and management, and received a certificate for completion of FBI Training School. He later became a member of the U.S. Coast Guard and was discharged in 1947. In 1950 he was recalled to active duty in the Korean War. During this tour of duty he was stationed at Hillsboro Inlet Light Station.

From 1952-57, Chuck became a part of Hillsboro Beach as the town's first patrolman, hired by Mayor French.

Chuck fondly remembers many of the residents, among them Ernest Wooler, who kept the engine he had designed for Rolls Royce in his living room. "Wooler was a fantastic engineer--unreachable--astonishing with his knowledge of science, an incredible perfectionist," recalls Chuck.

Kanode also remembers Clint King, who lived at 955 Hillsboro Mile. Having sold Coca Cola around the world during World War II, King's dream was to put Coke memorabilia in town hall. No one knows what happened to the dream.

After his stint as a police officer for Hillsboro Beach, Chuck was employed by King and other owners to maintain their properties and care for their exclusive homes in the area. In 1960 he purchased Community Loan in Pompano Beach and remained its president until 1973, when it was acquired by AVCO Finance.

Kanode is now retired and lives in Pompano Beach.

Those Who Came After

In November 1949, when Mayor Wooler proposed trading in his personal 1941 Studebaker Champion to purchase a police car for the town, his aim was that he, as mayor, and Amo Angeletti, as town marshal, would share it. The following year the purchase of the police car--with radio--was approved.

In 1956 The Barefoot Mailman restaurant was granted its liquor license and the town commission ruled that the 35 miles per hour speed limit was to be strictly enforced in Hillsboro Beach. Police car radio service was obtained under contract with Pompano Beach for $10 per month.

In June 1958, Raymond T. McMullin became acting town marshal; four months later, in October, he became town marshal. That year the town became equipped to time speed electrically, a camera was purchased for the fingerprinting department, new uniforms were purchased (including winter clothing), and an agreement with Pompano Beach was reached regarding housing of prisoners at $2.65 per day.

Chief McMullin was a resident of Deerfield Beach. His former neighbor, attorney George Patterson, recalls him as being a "great neighbor."

During McMullin's tenure--in 1963--the radar system which was used in the police car was donated by Mayor Alexander D. Henderson.

In July 1964, Chief McMullin reported to the town commission:

On June 22nd, 1964, a civil service examination was held in our town hall under the supervision of the civil service board members for the purpose of creating an eligibility list of men that would be acceptable as future police officers. Seven men participated in this examination. Stanley Manning averaged the highest score in this examination: 127.2. At the time the examination was given, Stanley Manning was already working as an auxiliary patrolman [Hillsboro Beach had Auxiliary Police until 1968] and my intention is to move Manning into the opening that was left vacant by the resignation of Thomas Millwood. Starting date for Stanley Manning will be August 1st, 1964. Starting rate of pay will be the usual starting amount, which will be $4,441 for the first year. Mr. Manning will also be placed on probation for this first year. The second highest score turned in was attained by Ralph Dunn: 113.2. Mr. Ralph Dunn is at the present time working as an auxiliary patrolman replacing Stanley Manning. . . .

There are two patrolmen in our department at the present time. These two patrolmen have completed their probationary period and are now accepted as full-fledged police officers. These officers' names are Charles Albro and Robert Sherman. These men in my opinion have done an outstanding job in the past year. Having worked on the auxiliary police for an additional year which gives them a total of a little more than two years service in our town. Therefore I would like to show my appreciation for a job well done by elevating them in rank to the title of corporal.

For the first time within the last five years I am pleased to be able to report to the commission members that the morale of the police officers in Hillsboro Beach is the highest it has ever been. There is no friction of any kind between or among the members of this department.

Personally, I am proud and honored to be the chief of police at Hillsboro Beach, and on any occasion I always speak very highly of our commissioners and the residents of this town. I have always thought that the people that live in Hillsboro Beach were of the highest caliber of people and that they were deserving of the finest police protection available. As the town grows and more policemen are necessary I shall insist that the men that are added will be honest, efficient, intelligent, and courteous.

* * *

In a letter to the town residents on November 7, 1964, Mayor Floyd Grainger made the following report regarding the police department:

> *Two retired policemen were employed as dispatchers at a nominal salary of $273 per month each so that our town hall could be opened 24 hours per day--seven days a week. Heretofore, the town hall closed at 4:00 P.M. each day and police officers on duty received calls through the city of*

Deerfield. We now have a radio and telephone dispatcher on duty at the town hall at all times to efficiently serve the residents and visitors and relay all calls to the police officers on duty. Effective October 1, 1964, the telephone number of the police department was changed to 399-6600 with two relay numbers (6601 and 6602) in the event 6600 [is] busy. Telephone stickers were forwarded on September 2nd by the police department.

* * *

In 1965 Hillsboro Beach granted the chief permission to purchase uniform traffic tickets as approved by the American Bar Association. Some of the fines assessed by the Hillsboro Beach police were:

5 to 10 mph over limit	$ 7.00
Improper passing	12.00
No muffler	12.00
Driving under influence/liquor or drugs	
Non-accident	202.00
Accident	301.00
Court costs, additional	2.00

On July 15, 1968, a memo went out to "All Hillsboro Beach Residents" from the "Waterway Committee Established by Town Commission."

SUBJECT: POLICE PATROL BOAT NOW IN COMMISSION

This is written to advise you that our newly acquired and equipped Police Boat is now operational and has officially begun service on our waterways for your added personal protection and that of your property.

On behalf of Mayor Truelson and all of our Commissioners, your Waterway Committee thanks all of our residents who contributed funds to our Town specifically for the activation of our Police Patrol Boat in accordance with the request contained in our letter of April 12, 1968.

Cash contributions to date amount to $3,813, compared to requested $2,950. This is an outstanding response from contributing citizens and the money has been placed in a special bank account and used for no other purpose than equipping the Police Boat.

As of today, after paying for a new 100 HP Mercury Outboard Engine and Controls plus a Motorola Police Radio installation, the police boat bank account balance is $1,466.88. Bills for various other required equipment items (i.e., electric megaphone, flashing red warning lights, fire extinguisher, life preservers, fenders, mooring whips, anchor and line and sign painting--"Hillsboro Beach Police") will further reduce the boat bank balance to a few hundred dollars. No town funds have been spent on the police boat to date.

Those who have not had an opportunity to participate in this most worthwhile and all around beneficial project may wish to send a contribution now.

* * *

On September 15, 1970, a tribute was paid to Chief McMullin on his retirement; Robert Sherman was named acting chief. That same fall, a special detective was hired to investigate break-ins, and a letter was sent to residents regarding burglar-proofing of homes.

In June 1971 the police department moved its quarters from town hall to the building behind it, which had once been the home of Amo Angeletti when he served as town marshal. An article by Linda Keating in the *Deerfield Beach Observer* describes their new offices:

> *The Police Department of Hillsboro Beach has moved their location from a confining room in Town Hall, out back to their ex-police chief's house.*
>
> *According to Police Chief Robert Sherman, the thirteen personnel on the Hillsboro force remodeled the home in their off duty hours. What was once a man's castle is now an attractive wood-paneled police headquarters. The accommodations are quite complete, from the detectives' office to the patrolmen's kitchen and locker room. The house also provides for a spacious reception room, as well as a cell area and large office for the Chief.*
>
> *The total cost of the project, including a new drive and equipment, was approximately $4500.*
>
> *Chief Sherman is extremely pleased with the result, and feels that the new conditions will mean a great difference in the department's efficiency, so watch out!*

* * *

In 1972 Chief Sherman was replaced by Acting Chief Ralph Dunn. An article in the *Deerfield Beach Observer* on June 6, 1974, described Chief Dunn and his observations:

HILLSBORO--A POLICEMAN'S PARADISE

> *It's a narrow strip of coast, peaceful, green, dotted with palm trees, often bathed in soft ocean breezes, and [it is] a policeman's paradise.*
>
> *[With] its high-rise and low-rise homes, [it is]*

a winter retreat for migrating snowbirds and the last stop for a few of the nation's wealthy elderly.

Still, Hillsboro Beach is a policeman's paradise, and the top cop is a former barber.

Ralph Dunn, 32, crew cut, married and a West Virginia transplant, does not know what makes an ex-barber turn policeman, but he did it, and he has been doing it for 10 years, the last three as chief.

"A little over 10 years ago, I got married on a Thursday in Bridgeport, West Virginia, arrived in Fort Lauderdale that Saturday and have been in Broward County ever since," he said.

Dunn had worked only a short time as a barber, and found himself employed as an electrician's helper when he first arrived in Fort Lauderdale.

"But I had to be outside, so I took a part time job as an auxiliary officer with the Hillsboro Beach police force," he said.

And part time soon became full time as out-doors in Hillsboro Beach became more and more comfortable.

Auxiliary officer, patrolman and chief, and Ralph Dunn has loved every bit of it.

"The most serious crimes--if you can call them that--have been vandalism. Once in a while, you get a case of breaking and entering, but such cases are few," he said. "There's no way I would trade the job unless it was to a similar community."

When Dunn first joined the force, there were seven officers, and now there are 14, including himself.

"Of course we have traffic problems, but there is only one street--Highway A1A," he said.

Dunn, playing down any criticism, said the

town--700 residents strong--has been accused of being a speed trap but termed it sheer tripe.

"Oh, they have said our men hide in the bushes waiting to pounce on unwary motorists," he said. "But that's not true.

"Sure they come out of driveways to catch someone speeding, but that is the only pavement in town other than A1A," he said.

Ten years on the force, and Chief Dunn (he is very thankful) has only been attacked once.

"I went to quell an apartment disturbance about five years ago and got charged by a 17-year-old with a screwdriver and high on pot," he said.

Fortunately, the chief was not hurt, and although the youth drove off in his own car, he was later caught in Deerfield Beach.

"Ninety-nine point nine percent of the time, though, the people of Hillsboro Beach are pleasant," he said.

"They are fantastic and constantly stopping to talk with you," Dunn said. "I wouldn't trade my job for the world."

And Chief Dunn, the top cop in Policeman's Paradise, means it.

* * *

However humble the police department may be, the Hillsboro police have had to deal with their share of problems--comparable to any small town on Florida's oceanfront. Throughout the town's existence, the police have handled a broad range of situations, from confrontations with gamblers, traffic offenders, turtle poachers, false alarms and numerous drownings--where they personally swam out into the ocean to save swimmers. They have also dealt with surfers trespassing on the town's private beaches, boats sinking, burglaries of homes and boats, and many of the refugees who have come in boats to the Florida coast.

Their dedicated service is renowned, and Hillsboro Beach residents take great pride in the police department. On August 15, 1983, one of the town's finest, 16-year police department veteran Police Lt. Robert H. Jones, was honored by a neighboring community, Deerfield Beach. An article in the Boca Raton *News* explained:

COP HONORED FOR FIREFIGHTING AT HILLSBORO CLUB

At the Deerfield Beach Fire Department's suggestion, the Town Commission last week commended Hillsboro Beach Police Lt. Robert H. Jones for his part in controlling a recent fire at the Hillsboro Club.

The officer risked his life containing a fire that could have caused substantial damage and imperiled lives, Deerfield Beach Battalion Chief Ed Coggin said in a letter to Hillsboro Beach Police Chief Ralph Dunn. Deerfield Beach answers fire calls under contract for the town, which has no fire department of its own.

"On the night of Friday, July 1, 1983, we received an alarm of a fire in the dining area of the Hillsboro Club," the letter said. "Upon arrival at the fire scene, I was advised that a Hillsboro Police Officer was on the second floor level on the east side of the building with a garden hose," the letter said.

Jones said the [Hillsboro Beach] Police Department received the alarm at about the same time [as the Deerfield Beach Fire Department] and he was at the scene shortly before the fire department and another Hillsboro Beach police officer John Ballar, who also answered the call.

"I got there first and, indeed, there was a fire on the east side of the dining room," Jones said. "I went around to the beach side and found the hose."

He also found a ladder used by construction workers and used it to climb to the roof.

"I had it pretty well contained by the time the Fire Department got there," Jones said. "They finally put it out completely."

Firefighters were about 10 minutes responding to the blaze, which Jones said is a good response time to the club, situated at the farthest point south in the town from the nearest Deerfield Beach Fire Department station. . . .

"Without the quick action of Lt. Jones, the second floor roof would have become involved and serious damage to this area would have caused physical damage to the sprinkler system," the letter continued. . . .

"Lt. Jones should be commended for his action," Coggins' letter went on. "He put [himself] in considerable jeopardy due to the unsafe conditions of the roof and a LP gas tank which was in the immediate area where Lt. Jones was using the garden hose in order to keep the fire in check until our arrival."

Jones, who has worked on the Hillsboro Beach police force 16 years, said his only fire fighting experience was basic fire training while he was with the U.S. Coast Guard. He did get first hand experience fighting fires while with the Coast Guard. He was called on to fight two fires--both of them at the Hillsboro Club.

* * *

Although keeping peace in Hillsboro Beach was not always the easiest of jobs, in 1995 Lt. Jones was still on duty, having been on the force for 28 years. The same year, Chief Dunn was honored for 30 years of service. Hillsboro Beach's title "Safest City in South Florida," had been achieved only through the great dedication of officers such as Dunn and Jones.

Once again, the *Deerfield Beach Observer*'s Judy Wilson summarized the sincerity and dedication of Hillsboro Beach's police department:

CITIES HONOR THEIR FINEST
DUNN: THREE DECADES OF "KEEPING PEACE" ON THE MILE

When Police Chief Ralph Dunn saw the notice for a special town meeting at a date and time the commission never convenes, he got nervous.

"I thought they were going to cut some benefits to the department," Dunn said, "and I was worried about some of the men here. Of course, I was going to be all right no matter what . . . I have my 30 years."

It turned out the "meeting" was all about the chief's 30 years and not about police benefits at all. The town's two dozen employees and five elected officials threw him a party last week commemorating his three decades of service.

"I never thought they would do something like that for me," he said.

Dunn is police chief in a town of 1,800 people, located on a three-mile stretch of state highway. In 1993 it was the FBI's safest city in South Florida. No violent crime. Only five property crimes.

"This is a place where the men come to work in a clean shirt and leave the same way," Dunn says

of what might be called a bucolic lifestyle for a police officer.

Dunn, 53, joined the department in 1964 as an auxiliary officer. The next year he became a sworn officer and in 1972, police chief. When he came to this town there were about 600 people and the tallest building was three stories.

In those days, a policeman's chief duty in Hillsboro Beach was to check up on residences, most of them occupied only in the winter. "We're still doing it," Dunn said. "It's still one of our main jobs." That, and answering sick calls. "The Deerfield EMS does a terrific job, but our cars still carry oxygen and all our men are trained in CPR and first aid."

If cops and robbers are your preference, don't expect to be a law enforcement officer in Hillsboro Beach. Even household burglaries are down with the advent of inexpensive, sophisticated alarm systems, Dunn said. He scratches his head to remember the last violent crime--1992, he thinks--a robbery and assault.

In the late '80s there were five traffic deaths in one year, a memorable statistic, because for the previous 13 years there had been none. There has never been a murder.

In keeping with the times, if crime is increasing in Hillsboro Beach, it is with domestic violence complaints. "Not among the homeowners," Dunn hastens to explain, "but we're getting more young renters. Of course, it's still not a lot, maybe five a year, but it's more than before."

Does working for a community of wealthier-than-usual people come with unusual demands? "Absolutely not," the chief said. "Most of our residents come here for privacy, rest and relaxation.

And that's what we try to give them. When they're away we check the house three times a day. When they are here, we just drive by and wave."

Hillsboro's oldest employee in terms of service looks back on his career with satisfaction. In all that time he had only eight or nine months when he thought his job might be on the line. The situation was a mayor (now deceased) and a personality conflict that pitted the two "like tom cats in a dark alley," Dunn remembers. "But I've been very fortunate with my bosses. They have said to me, 'Hey, it's your baby. If you have a problem, call me.'"

Dunn, in fact, is the information source for the town, a responsibility he shoulders willingly. "I'm expected to know everything," he says modestly, "and after all these years, I should."

Last week at Dunn's surprise luncheon, party planners David Denman, the city clerk, and his staff, Darlene Pfister and Irene George, strung banners at the Deerfield Beach Resort that offered both wise cracking condolences and congratulations. His wife, Joyce, was there. To Dunn's amazement she kept the party a secret.

He describes his main emotion as "relief" when he discovered the special meeting was a luncheon rather than a lynching.

Dunn and Joyce have lived in Deerfield Beach for 32 years, in the same house. The future for them may include more time in North Carolina where they have a home outside of Franklin, but Dunn is reluctant to predict his next five years.

"It's just very hard to say if I'll be here or not. This city gives me a free hand. It's been awfully easy."

* * *

11

The Water Department

In 1947, Ernest Wooler wrote in his diary:

Water continues to be a problem. Pompano has not installed the 6-inch submarine pipe that was suggested. Water comes from a fire hose, since the 4-inch main was broken a year ago. Please repair 4-inch main so that the water does not have to be cut off every time the bridge across the inlet is opened.

* * *

On October 30, 1947, officials in Pompano suggested that Hillsboro Beach obtain its water service from Deerfield Beach because of the sands, currents, and dredging of the inlet. The following year, Wooler proposed that drilling be attempted directly west of the town for water.

The problems with the town's water situation was ongoing. Pressure was non-existent, and water was hoarded because it was so undependable. In 1949 Wooler sent a card to all residents giving them a choice between three alternatives: 1) the town's own water plant at a cost of $50,000, 2) a contract with Deerfield Beach, 3) a contract with Pompano Beach and $15,000 for a new main. The third option was adopted.

Thirty water bond certificates were sold at $500 each. Surnames of those holding the bonds were: Small, White, Pierson, French, Cordes, Freidt, Sherman, Carpenter, Wellington, King (John and Janet), Shethar, Stradella, Malcolm and Parry.

Water was carried across the inlet frequently by a fire hose which ran across the bridge, and it had to be disconnected every time the bridge opened. It was clear that there needed to be a replacement for the old water main, a rubber hose which ran under the inlet to Pompano Beach.

Wooler visited Pompano Beach City Hall, obtaining the minute books to check the ordinances regarding the water pipe. The present pipe was inadequate--no more than a makeshift job--for it was subject to corrosion and frequent damage from the strong current of tide water under the bridge. Some homeowners at the north end of town got their water from Deerfield Beach until January 1953.

In 1949, homeowners on the west side of the Intracoastal Waterway had petitioned Hillsboro Beach for annexation rather than become part of Deerfield Beach or Pompano Beach. It was then that there began discussions about obtaining a water well in this area. A petition was sent to Tallahassee and was properly advertised, then passed the House and the Senate. However, it was stonewalled via political influence from Deerfield Beach.

With the aid of Town Marshal Amo Angeletti and the town jeep, Wooler removed the pipe in the inlet. Replacing it would have been only a temporary solution, so Hillsboro Beach pursued the idea of having its own water plant.

A 20-acre parcel of land was secured on Sample Road near the railroad tracks, about two miles from the town. A high water tank was erected by Chicago Bridge and Iron Company for $37,950 and two small wells were drilled. Each well supplied 250 gallons per minute. A 10-inch water line to the town was installed under Sample Road. The water was good, passed all health requirements and was adequate for quite a while.

Later a third well of 1200 gallons per minute was installed to take care of increased demands. Some additional water lines were installed in the town, as well as water meters. A booster pump was provided to increase the pressure. This also was sufficient for some time, but the water began to show rust or iron content. In 1965 it became apparent that there was just not enough water in the town at certain times to cater to the demands of the increasing population. Two bond issues were passed in 1966. One provided $100,000 for fire equipment and the other $750,000 for water expansion. Both were validated by the court but were later canceled by the commissioners. However, the town had enough money to put in another 1200-gallon well and proceeded to do so.

In 1968 a new eight-inch water pipe was installed along the east side of A1A. This necessitated the removal of all sod, ground cover, shrubbery, rocks, cement bumpers, signs, mailboxes and lamp posts six feet east of the pavement.

In 1971 a new water filtration plant was in operation. By 1972 there were 26 hydrants along Hillsboro Mile--including two on private property, the Hillsboro Club, and one on U.S. Coast Guard property. Commissioner Shaffer recommended that six more be installed.

In 1977 Hillsboro Beach's water plant was recognized with a first place award for its effectiveness and as a first class facility in state competition. The credit behind the award-winning operation of the water treatment plant went to Water Superintendent M.D. Jones.

An easement had been granted to Broward County years earlier, and the funds which accrued because of it were still available. In 1979 the roads to the water plant were repaved with those funds.

Mainco, Inc., was hired in March 1981 to paint and clean the water plant. The cost to the town was $52,427. Later that year a water truck was purchased from King Oldsmobile for $6,159.75.

Emergency services have been exchanged with Deerfield Beach throughout the years. In 1979 Hillsboro Beach serviced the beach area of Deerfield Beach during a water break. In 1981, Deerfield Beach provided water to Hillsboro Beach while repairs were being made on the town's water tank.

A new era came to the town's water treatment plant with the acceptance of fluoridation. On March 29, 1982, under the headline "Fluoridated Water To Reach Hillsboro," the *Fort Lauderdale Sun-Sentinel*'s Elizabeth Roberts wrote:

> *Hillsboro Beach residents will be drinking fluoridated water by this fall and it won't cost them a cent--at least not for two years.*
>
> *The city has received an $11,239 federal grant which will pay for the initial cost of the system and its operation for two years.*
>
> *After that, it will cost the city about $800 a year to run the system, according to Eldrod Wilson, the city's water plant superintendent.*
>
> *The U.S. Department of Health and Human Services is offering grants to communities throughout the state as an incentive to fluoridate the water, said Linda Greis, the project coordinator of the*

grant program. The city of Fort Lauderdale is also installing a fluoridation system as part of its $2 million water plant expansion project. That system was funded in part with a $100,000 federal grant, said Tom Mueller of the county's health department.

With the completion of the Fort Lauderdale and Hillsboro Beach systems, the number of county residents drinking fluoridated water will increase from 55 percent to about 75 percent, Mueller said.

It is doubtful, however, the county will reach its goal of having all residents drinking fluoridated water. . . .

"Fluoride's main benefit is in preventing cavities in children. With older people they find it plays a role in preventing bones from becoming brittle," [Greis] said.

"Many adults in Hillsboro Beach come from up North where they were already drinking fluoridated water," Ms. Greis added. . . .

Wilson said Hillsboro Beach's water department has begun to dig the foundation for the system, which has a life expectancy of 15 to 25 years.

Residents will pay between 20 and 40 cents each year to keep the system operating after the federal grant is discontinued in two years, Ms. Greis said. . . .

* * *

Since the program went into effect in 1980, 13 communities in the state have taken advantage of it.

Also in 1982, Hillsboro Beach obtained an easement from the First Christian Church of Pompano Beach for the purpose of locating, drilling and maintaining a salt water intrusion monitoring test well on a portion of the water plant property.

By 1984 the water plant needed modernizing. The firm of Camp, Dresser and McKee, Inc., was interviewed to draw up specific tasks the town needed to have done and provide a cost estimate. One of the first tasks to be addressed was the creation of a plan for the replacement of existing cement-asbestos pipes with an iron-cast type. The advantage of the latter: it could bend rather than break. In addition the firm was asked to plan a building for the utility department's use. A combination garage and storage building would house the department's two trucks and a tractor and give the employees a place to work. The firm was also asked to design and install a master meter to record the flow of water from the plant.

Repairs, additions and maintenance have gone on throughout the last decade. Today Rodney Main, the town's superintendent of water utilities, has announced that the 1,000 feet of concrete pipe at the north end of town must be replaced. Those pipes are thirty years old. The town's water account has a fund of $1.5 million that can be used for such expenses.

12

Hurricanes and Erosion

An extremely violent, whirling, spiraling tropical cyclone-- shaped somewhat like a funnel--frequently originates in tropical regions of the North Atlantic Ocean, Caribbean Sea, Gulf of Mexico and eastern North Pacific Ocean. Result: a hurricane.

This definition from the Division of Marine and Environmental Systems at the Florida Institute of Technology can be applied to other names, as well, depending upon its location. These tropical cyclones are called typhoons in the western North Pacific Ocean, hurricanes in the eastern North Pacific, baguios in the South China Sea, cyclones in the Indian Ocean and willy-willies in Australia. By any name, they bring terror.

Wind speeds must be 74 miles per hour or greater to be classified as a hurricane. The direction of rotation of wind in a hurricane is counterclockwise in the northern hemisphere and clockwise in the southern hemisphere. The average hurricane's center, referred to as the eye, is about 14 miles in diameter. The eye is surrounded by hurricane force winds, and is known as the wall cloud, or eye wall. Outside the wall, winds decrease fairly rapidly to tropical storm or gale force.

The Florida Experience

The hurricane season for the North Atlantic area occurs during the months of June through November, with September having the greatest number. It is then that winds, flooding, torrential rainfall, storm surges--the abnormal rise in sea level--all can become life threatening. A cubic yard of seawater weighs nearly three-fourths of a ton and promises destruction of anything in its path. Except when crossing flat, wet areas as they do in South Florida, hurricanes usually weaken rapidly as they move inland.

From 1493 to 1870, the Caribbean area and Florida experienced nearly 400 hurricanes which were reported by Professor E.B. Garriot in 1900 in his classic study, *West Indian Hurricanes*.

From 1872-1993, nearly a thousand tropical cyclones of tropical storm or hurricane intensity have occurred in the North Atlantic, Caribbean Sea and Gulf of Mexico. Of these, nearly 180 have reached Florida, with 75 known to have hurricane-force winds (74 mph) and 105 with tropical storm-force winds (39-73 mph).

On September 22, 1848, the acknowledged "granddaddy of all Florida hurricanes," struck the state's west coast with a fury it has never known since. Lighthouses such as the one on Edmont Key toppled like match sticks, homes were flattened, whole islands disappeared, and large ships were swept in and smashed to pieces on the mainland.

Beaches were strewn with wreckage and valuables: furniture, barrels of whiskey, wood, farm and household equipment were left on the beaches as tokens of misery. In ensuing years this scene has been repeated many times along Florida's coasts.

Monsters in South Florida

In September 1926 a monstrous storm hit South Florida, nearly destroying the real estate boom. Just east of the Miami Canal at Sebring Farm, 63 people huddled in their biggest farmhouse. The surging waters destroyed the house and only six people survived. Further east, 34 people took refuge in a dairy barn and only two of them escaped drowning.

Property loss in the Miami district was estimated at $13 million. Ten thousand homes were unroofed, and 75 people were known dead. Relief poured in from organizations and individuals across the nation.

Two years later, horrified residents recalled the big Miami hurricane when a monster storm hit the Lake Okeechobee region without warning, leaving 2,000 dead. A true "killer," it had smashed through Puerto Rico two days earlier, leaving hundreds dead or homeless.

On Sunday--September 16, 1928--the weather bureau reported that the big wind would pass far clear of the region, and everyone began to relax. Yet something was wrong, particularly the stillness, as the monster storm veered westward. Too late were the warning calls from West Palm Beach just before the lines went down. Too late--for there were no roads south and west and, therefore, no way out.

By six o'clock that Sunday evening, darkness had come, and with it the terror of howling winds and sharp rain. Houses were blown away and trees and cars jostled the streets. Winds reached 160 miles per hour and the lake's waters poured 22 miles of muck along the south shore of the lake.

Fort Lauderdale's first builder, Ed King, who lived at the lake, huddled in John Aunapu's packing house on Torrey Island. He died with eleven others, struck by a timber while trying to save two children.

People watched while their homes and the bodies of neighbors and strangers floated by. A section of dike flooded and obliterated the little town of Moore Haven, killing about 150 people.

After the longest of nights, dreadful days followed in what became the greatest natural disaster in Florida's history and--aside from Galveston and Johnstown--the greatest in the country.

In Belle Glade, families found shelter in the town's two hotels, the Glades and the Belle Glades. Others found shelter in sturdy canal barges, but many elected to stay in their homes.

The first blast struck in a pitch black night; one could not see even his own raised hand, nor a sound above the roaring. Shelters were ripped to pieces and people clutched at anything, including chains of humans, linked hand in hand.

At 10:00 P.M., all stopped. The noise and winds became a deafening silence, and people shivered with dread--feeling, rather than knowing--the worst was yet to come. There was only blackness. Within a short time Belle Glade's streets were seven feet under water. South Bay, Bean City, Pahokee and other settlements were gone. The dike, like a huge bucket of water, had broken and water had risen eleven feet in some places. Hundreds had been caught up in the raging waters, clinging to whatever was in their paths, sometimes for miles.

As people scrambled, they were faced with another menace. The army of venomous semi-aquatic water moccasins and poisonous snakes, also seeking shelter, outnumbered humans by 10,000 to one. Many died from snake bites; others endured painful anti-venom treatment later.

The disaster had respect for no earthly being nor possession. Nearly every road and bridge had been swept away and made rescue efforts impossible. Word of the tragedy did not reach West Palm Beach until the next day, and work had to begin with the temporary repair of the roads and waterways.

The first to arrive were the Red Cross teams. But the worst of tasks began immediately: rounding up all the drowning victims. Anyone with tools worked around the clock making coffins from salvaged wood. So many bodies were found at times that making coffins was futile. Funeral pyres had to be used and were a reminder to the survivors for many days.

The final estimate of deaths was more than 2,000, but that figure is considered short, for skeletons were found for years afterward in the surrounding area.

Damage was estimated at $25 million. In the aftermath, President Hoover approved construction of a vast stone levee 34 to 38 feet high and 85 miles around the lake's southern end. One hopes it will never have to be tested.

In 1933 two hurricanes entered the east coast of Florida within a short distance of each other. The property loss in Indian River, St. Lucie and Palm Beach Counties probably was about $2 million.

Again in 1935, two hurricanes visited South Florida. More than 400 people drowned. The Flagler Railroad tracks were washed from the Long Key viaduct. A rescue train sent to the Keys to transport residents was swept from the tracks by the storm.

By the 1940s the use of "hurricane-hunter" planes had begun. However, the radio silence required during World War II over the Atlantic stifled these efforts, and few weather reports were received from ships at sea. Ten hurricanes were reported in 1943-45.

A Hurricane Comes to Hillsboro Beach

On September 17, 1947--when hurricanes still had no identifying names--there came a category 4 hurricane which, except for Hurricane Andrew 45 years later, had the highest recorded wind speed in Florida's history. It registered a one-minute maximum windspeed of 155 miles per hour. This was recorded at the Hillsboro Lighthouse. The barometric pressure reached 27.97 inches of mercury at Hillsboro and tides were recorded at Clewiston and Moore Haven of 21.6 and 20.9 feet.

Fifty-one people died in the 1947 hurricane. By that time, many people had barometers that they watched carefully. A large number of residents had become storm conscious, keeping canned foods and batteries on hand and putting up storm shutters. Many chose to receive inoculation against typhoid. In Fort Lauderdale the U.S. Naval Air Station was set up as a refuge station that could be used during disasters.

In December 1947 Ernest and Gertrude Wooler sent their annual Christmas greetings to family and friends. It was the "Hurricane Log of 1947." The data and sketches were done by Ernest and the narrative by Gertrude. This diary describes the storm, the preparations, fears and relief that people endured through these disasters.

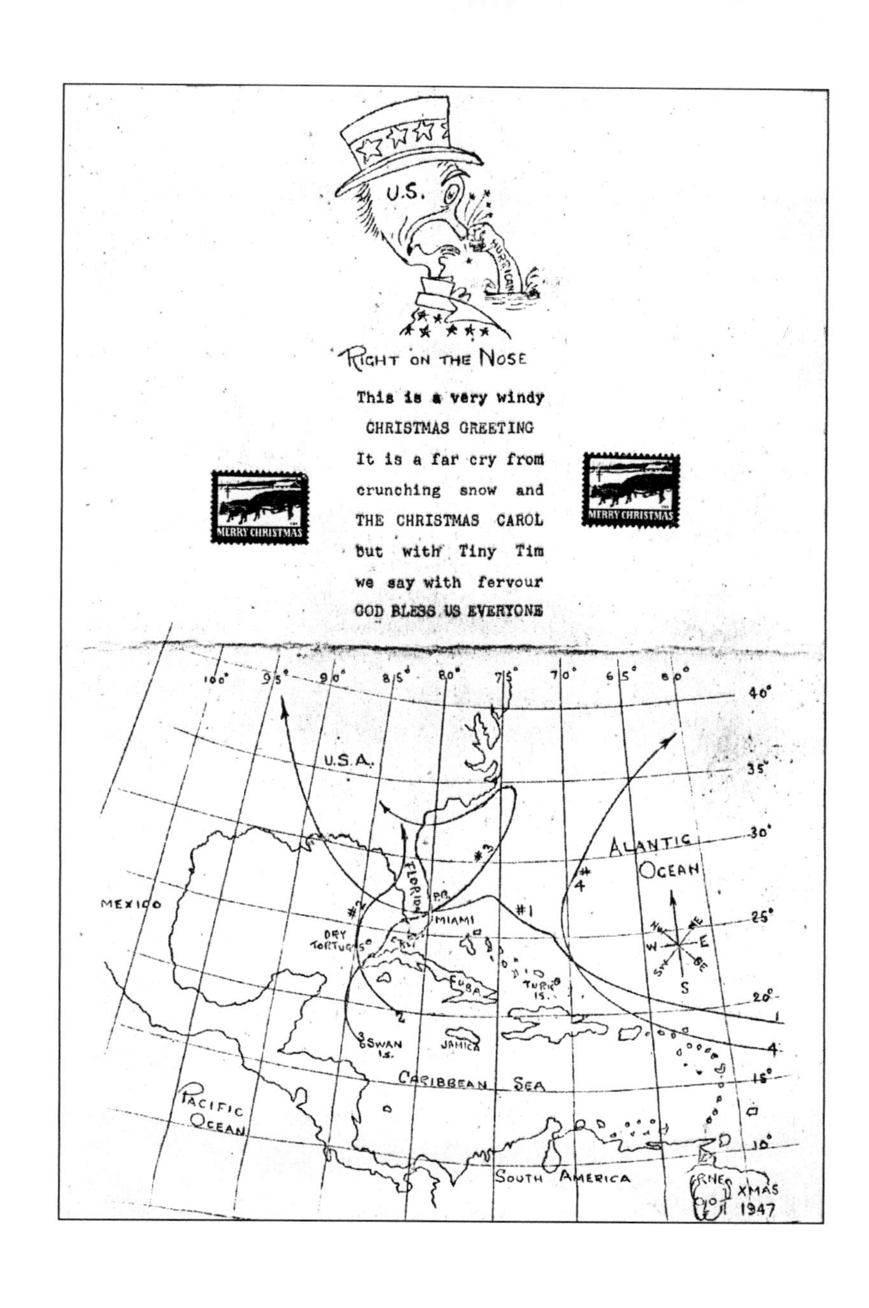

HURRICANE LOG--1947

[the Woolers' Christmas Greeting]

We live half a mile north of the Hillsboro Inlet, on the south east coast of Florida. Hillsboro Mile, as it is called, is a ridge twenty-five feet above high tide. The "Mile" varies in width. Where we are, it is 400 feet from the Atlantic Ocean on the east to the Intra-coastal Waterway on the west.

Our house is built into the hills. Two stories overlook the garden, drive, highway and waterway on the west. From the beach on the east it is a low one-story house, although very little of it can be seen, as we have not disturbed the natural beach growth. From the sun deck on the roof, we can look out on a world of waters, with the purple Gulf Stream only a mile or two from the shore. The Hillsboro Light swings its great beam over the sea from sunset to sunrise. The trade winds blow gentle, sweet and cool. Dramatic processions of clouds attend the Gulf Stream.

We often wondered what the gentle breeze would be like if it became a gale, or worse, a hurricane--that evil spirit! Then we would reassure ourselves by talking of our solidly built, reinforced concrete house on its sturdy foundations. A house built high above the ocean--25 feet in southern Florida is high--and protected by 100 feet of heavy foliage, seagrape, yucca and palmetto. The tide? It is a mere two-foot rise when we have waves.

We have lived here two years, and the first spring we did get a little scare when a heavy northeast ground swell sneaked up and up the beach, and smoothly and softly washed away six feet of our vegetation. We thought our beach steps would go. The concrete block at the foot hung on the steps and handrail. All this is just one high tide.

Ern made a platform of driftwood at the top of the steps, partly as another place to sit and look out to sea, but mostly to anchor the steps to solid ground. During the summer the sea built up the sand again and covered the concrete block. The platform grew into a cute little cabana with a tilted palmetto roof, which we called "The Straw Hat." We used it a lot. We take our work down there. We had lunch there. My sister Jeannette spent her entire holiday there, except when she was rushing to the doctor with a new case of sunburn. The sunburn was my fault, as I took her for a long walk on the beach the first day she was here. Very foolish of me. It is hard to get over a bad burn.

Most people know Florida only in the wintertime, with its balmy climate and sunny days, but think it would be too hot in the summer. We know how delightful it really is--never above 90 all summer, and always the Trade Winds blowing cool and perfumed from the Ocean.

We Wait to See How the Wind Blows

As the Autumnal Equinox approaches, we wonder if Florida will escape a blow. Every year it is the same. There are many conflicting opinions. Some say that because of the wet summer we won't have a storm. Others say for that very reason we will have a storm. John Muskrat, the Seminole, prophesies bad weather, but Jim Running Deer says hunting will be good. So, there you are.

We have often said, we wouldn't wish for one, but if one occurred, we'd like to see a hurricane. We have changed our minds. The wet summer has made our place perfectly beautiful. No, definitely, we don't want a storm. We don't ever want to see one. In the past fifty years, this section of Florida has never been directly hit by a hurricane.

The first week in September. Over the radio comes the report that a tropical disturbance has been discovered in the Doldrums, 2,000 miles away. This specter moves like a shadow through every radio report.

Sept. 13, 1947. The Miami Weather Bureau advises that the disturbance is now a small hurricane, and that it is moving northwesterly. It is away out somewhere east of Nassau. Our barometer is the usual 30.00, temperature 82. The ocean is a smooth, transparent Aquarelle. Swimming is delightful. White shells lie clear and quiet on the ocean floor. It is like swimming in a dream--cool and translucent.

Sept. 14, Sunday. This is our only lazy day. Breakfast on the west patio. The great sweeping fronds of the young palms sway gently in the light breeze. Great clusters of seagrapes are beginning to turn pink, and here and there a faint purple. There will be lots of seagrape jelly this year. The Hibiscus is an explosion of color. Before us is the culmination of summer, sun and rain--pushing, exuberant growth; exultant, riotous color.

The ocean is as smooth and clear as yesterday. We swim and walk to the lighthouse at the inlet and swim again.

Sept. 15, Monday. A beautiful sunny day with a light wind. Weather reports are reassuring. Blow believed heading north and out to sea. On the strength of the encouraging weather reports, our good friend and neighbor, Ruth Markland, has decided to follow through with her plans to go north to visit her family. We are taking her to the train at Boca Raton. Ruth is leaving her three little Dachshunds at home in the care of a young couple who will stay there until she returns.

Monday afternoon. The yard man is cleaning up the beach. The picnic grill is dismantled, and the blocks buried in the sand along the vegetation line, about 100 feet from the ocean. Benches and tables are stowed away, the beach raked. The water is just as clear, but a little rougher than yesterday. We add a few more shells to the mosaic around the cabana. The cabana itself has been freshly painted, and the palmetto thatch rustles pleasantly.

Sept. 16--up at 7 A.M. Turned on the radio. "North

Florida Alerted for Storm." "Hurricane 170 miles off Palm Beach. Expect recurve to the North." Breakfast on the west patio as usual. We wait to see how the wind blows! The sea is fairly smooth with ground swells. At 9:30 (high tide) sea getting rougher with white caps and long breakers reaching up to where the grill was yesterday. We have had 100 feet of beach all summer, and an average 2-foot tide. At low tide, we can walk out over 300 feet on the sand bar, and be only shoulder deep in water.

Gusty winds all morning, but not bad--a few rain drops. Ern is painting the south wall, and is glad of the cloudiness.

2:45 P.M. A shocking announcement! Weather advisory issues definite hurricane warnings! I called Chief Bennett of the Coast Guard at the lighthouse. He confirmed the warnings. We must get the shutters up at once. I jumped in my car and went to Pompano to find our yard man, John. I had his address. I could find no such place in colored town, and no one had ever heard of John. I found out afterward that his name is J.V., not John. Just J.V.

It was getting late, and I was getting more or less frantic, cruising back and forth over the rutty roads of colored town looking for John. Finally, in desperation, I yelled to a big six-footer. He ambled over to the car. "We must get our storm shutters up at once. There is a hurricane coming. Will you come to the shore and help us?"

Thank heaven, he was as good as his word. The storm shutters are up. There are screws missing here and there, but they are up. He and Ern are putting everything loose, including the straw part of The Straw Hat, in the garage. It is after dark. We are working like mad, and the strain is terrible. It may be all for nothing, but it has to be done.

8:45 P.M.--Weather Bureau Advisory--Storm center 160 miles east of Palm Beach. Moving due west at 8 mph. Good Heavens, it is really coming! It is out there in the dark, that concentration of mad energy, beside which the atomic bomb pales in its power of destruction. This evil thing, born in the Doldrums, and gaining in intensity every minute, is advancing on us at eight miles per hour!

The wind is blowing hard with stronger puffs. It has been gradually increasing all afternoon. Our barometer has dropped from 30.00 to 29.70.

10:00 P.M.--Chief Bennett called. Ern answered the phone. He told Ern he had been instructed to evacuate all people on the coast in his area. Ern told him he preferred to stay here in our own house. (I did not know this at the time.)

Ruth called from Pittsburgh, where she had just arrived. We told her we were here alone, and that the hurricane was coming. The people who were in her house have taken her car, her three dogs, their dog and left--literally gone with the wind.

10:45 P.M.--Weather Bureau Advisory--Storm 145 miles east of Palm Beach. Winds at center of hurricane reported to be 100 MPH. Our barometer is still 29.70. Northwest wind 30 mph. Sea at high tide, 9:50 P.M., was up to the beach cabana steps and building up sand. Some debris on beach. Intracoastal Waterway is higher than we have ever seen it--just below road level.

We are dead tired. Ern has decided to turn in. I am not going to bed--I couldn't sleep. As it turned out, Ern couldn't either.

12:45--Weather Bureau Advisory--Center of storm located at Lat. 26.5, N., Long. 77.9--130 miles east of Delray.

Our exact location is Lat. 26°-16'-17"N., Long. 80°-04'-48" W. Barometer 29.62 and falling fast. Ern has gone back to bed. I am going too.

Sept. 17--Something must have crashed against the

house, for at exactly 6 A.M. I sat straight up in bed and yelled "Here it is!" It was dark. We immediately got up. The lights were still on, but flickering, and going out altogether now and then. Terrific gales are battering the house from the northwest. Ern threw on some clothes, went out and put missing screws in the shutters--those that were neglected last night. He was soaked to the skin immediately. The sea is a mass of white foam filled with debris. The waterway is a Niagara rushing south, but not much higher than last night.

The sheets of rain are horizontal and full of sand. The water seems to be about up to the beach steps. Planks and debris are wedged under the platform. Suddenly, it is all lifted up--planks, debris, platform railings, concrete blocks, everything, to sail whirling and smashing down the beach. Ern came in, changed his clothes and insisted on going out again. He crawled up on [the] deck on his hands and knees, clinging to the railing to keep from being blown out to sea. The wind is getting stronger and wilder every minute. It is impossible to see anything.

My sister Win called from Cleveland, terribly excited, and begged us to leave. I tried to get hold of Chief Bennett. The line is busy. Ern feels safer in our own house anyway.

The lights went off permanently at 7 A.M. I made coffee on a sterno. We are not hungry.

8:45--Weather Bureau Advisory--very severe hurricane. Stay indoors. Wind at West Palm Beach 82-110 mph, Miami 55 mph. Our barometer 28.95, temp. 78°, relative humidity, 55.

9:30 A.M.--Barometer 28.82. The wind is worse. The house is dark. We can see just enough to walk without falling over things. We have all the closet doors open, so that air from the vents in the ceiling will circulate through the house. On the east side of the house we also have a window open a little. This to keep the pressure equalized inside, to keep the windows from being blown out.

The big mirror over the fireplace is puffing and pulling back and forth. It will be a terrible thing if that crashes. We'll be cut. We pull and push chairs together, pile one on top of the other. Ern has propped a dry mop against the glass, and wedged it on the top chair.

We must move all the furniture into the middle of the room. Water is coming in under the hall door on the west, and under the dining room door on the east. Towels! More towels! We're mopping up water and wringing it into pails. It's spreading over the floor! Is it the ocean? Is the ocean coming in?

The noise is stupefying! The roar of the ocean is louder than any thunder. It is deeper in tone and continuous. It is just outside the door! Banshees ride the screaming wind. Gusts hit the house like blows from great fists. The house shakes. Can it take it? Beneath the roar of the ocean and the shriek of the wind there is a moaning, and a groaning: lamenting of dead sailors drowned in long dead hurricanes? Who can tell?

10:00 A.M. Battery radio set is very weak. No weather report. We have no light, no water, no telephone.

Barometer, 28.72; Temperature 78°; R.H. 55.

11:00 A.M. Barometer 28.6

11:30 A.M. Barometer 28.5

11:45 A.M. The lull. We are in the eye of the hurricane. the wind has almost died down. The sun is even out a little--pale, timid and ashamed.

Ern went out during the lull. I could not bear to look at the havoc. The sea is up to our walk, almost on a level with the house, and only about 45 feet away. The road beside the waterway has disappeared, and under three feet of water. The waterway is half way up our west slope--a roaring torrent rushing down to the inlet.

12:00 Noon. The lull is over. We are on the northern perimeter of the eye. Note--At Fort Lauderdale the lull lasted for an hour and fifteen minutes, as it was in the exact center of the storm. We, and all the places north of us, up to Palm Beach, took the worst licking. They say here that the northern part of a storm is always the worst.

It has started all over again. Blowing Great Guns! Roaring, shrieking, moaning. It is from the opposite direction now--from the southeast. All our poor palms, hibiscus, seagrape, everything, which has been lying flat before the northwest wind is now screwed around in implacable crazy fists, and lies broken before the south-east squalling fury.

This is worse than the morning. It isn't possible, but there it is. It is worse. The roar of the sea is louder, the wind stronger, the gusts more furious. This morning, when I couldn't take any more, I sat in the S.W. corner of the S.W. bedroom, as far away from the noise and the storm as I could get. Now I am in Ern's office, which is on the west side in the middle of the house. I am near panic. Water is pouring in under the doors--I know it is sea water. Heavy, invisible objects are crashing against the house. The ocean is getting nearer every minute. Ern has to do the bailing alone. We aren't getting any weather reports--our battery is too low. It is dark as night. The pressure is exhausting, like being on a high mountain.

12:30 P.M. Barometer 28.6. Up a tenth. Thank God!

12:45 P.M. Battery set working, very low. Fort Lauderdale reported eye of storm at 11:48 A.M. Winds, reported, 155-165 mph.

Barometer at Miami, low 28.75. Ours 28.5.

1 P.M. Barometer 28.65 Temp. 81.

1:30 P.M. Barometer 28.75. Very dark. Hard driving rain. Hurricane winds. Temp. 82.

2 P.M. Barometer 28.95. Letting up a little. Rain and hurricane winds a little lighter. Terrible roar somewhat abated.

2:45 P.M. Barometer 29.00 Temp. 82. Still blowing great guns from SE or SW. Air full of sand. Solar system glass all over lawn. Canal water still over road, but one foot lower. Devastation reminiscent of blitz over London. Solar system ruined. Ern turned off water, as a precaution. Water already shut off at Pompano main. Impossible to go around to the east side--the ocean side.

4:00 P.M. Barometer still 29.00. Gale winds SSW.

5:30 P.M. We went out. Water down, but the road is floating on top of the water. Bent like rubber ice when stepped on. Dinner in dining room by oil lamp light. Weak tea made on sterno.

6:00 P.M. Barometer 29.15. Temp. 82.

7:00 P.M. Barometer 29.20. No more advisories apparently. The nervous strain has been terrific. We are gong to bed. The roar of the sea is not so pleasant to listen to tonight. There is still a gale blowing, and the ocean still sounds dangerous and very close. We realize now why the Coast Guard told us to evacuate. If the waves had been ten feet higher or we ten feet lower, we might have been washed out to sea. Our house certainly would have been undermined.

It has been a fearful day, and we so utterly isolated. The ocean only a few feet from us, waves 20 feet high tearing our land away, and on the other side, the waterway, a raging torrent overflowing its banks and covering the road three feet deep. We were indeed marooned.

Sept. 18, Thursday. Barometer 29.80, temp. 80.

Cloudy and still blowing hard from the SE. Air still full of sand. Breakfast--coffee (on sterno), eggs, bread (no toast) and butter and jam.

9:00 A.M.-12 Noon. Barometer normal, 30.00. We went on a tour of inspection. What a scene of desolation! Seagrape, palms, hibiscus, pines, telegraph poles, all flat and scattered about in mad disorder or gone entirely.

Here and there, as if in mockery, a tall palm stands, straight and easy with all its coconuts still clinging to it.

Our house is completely sandblasted, and coated an inch thick with sand and leaves. Great piles of sand are banked on the terraces and against the house. Every window crack is filled with it. The solar heater must be replaced and the house repainted, but aside from these two things, the house suffered very little damage.

The great shock, however, was walking down our ocean path. Forty-five feet from the house it ends and there is a fifteen foot drop straight down to the sand below. Great tangles of roots lie exposed. We lowered a ladder so that we could get down to the beach. We have a dog whose name is Napoleon. He is a French Poodle, and he loves the beach. He was completely unprepared for the great change that took place overnight in his scheme of things. The steps were here when he last went down on the beach and now they ain't. I climbed down the ladder and said, "Jump, Nap." After a little urging, he jumped and we went down the beach. When we came back, I put his front feet on the ladder and boosted him, then put his back feet on the ladder. He got the idea at once, and from then on Nap has gone up the ladder. He not only goes up the ladder, he also goes down it. His manner is, "Poooh, that's nothin'."

Here I'll leave a space for a drawing, to give you an idea of before and after the hurricane.

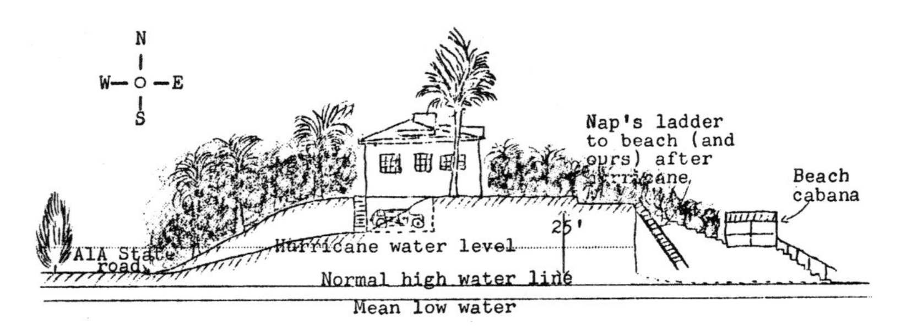

Our neighbor to the north had a number of windows blown in and great patches of tile swept from the roof. The water damage is great. The damage to the house of our neighbor to the south is very great. The house is undermined and two wings stick out into space with nothing under them but ocean. Great cracks run along the walls.

From Hillsboro Inlet to Boca Raton Inlet, the sea took from 50 feet to 100 feet all along the shore. At Deerfield, the small town just north of us, nine small houses were completely swept away. Here and there a house on piles stands on its little legs right in the ocean. People who had recently bought oceanfront lots woke up Thursday morning to find there was nothing there.

I went into Fort Lauderdale this afternoon to phone my sisters in Cleveland. We have no phone, no water, no electricity. No luck in Fort Lauderdale, either. Wires all down. Sent a letter, also a telegram without much hope of its ever getting there. (It got there, but it took a day or so.)

Sept. 19. Lovely day. Water on at 4:00 P.M.

Sept. 21. Second hurricane.

Turned on radio at 11:00 A.M. Advisory of second storm developing near Cuba. Wearily we put shutters over big window again.

6:00 P.M. Barometer 29.85, temp. 82. Strong winds. Storm clouds. However, we didn't get this one. I don't know where it went, and I don't care.

We were without electricity for eight days and without a phone for twelve days.

Third Hurricane

Oct. 10, 4:30 P.M. Weather Bureau Advisory. Florida west coast alerted. Storm warnings from Daytona Beach, south. Disturbance 125 miles SSW of the Dry Tortugas, proceeding NE at 15-18 MPH.

We are not too concerned about this one. A little blasé, maybe, but more especially because it is far to the west of us. The west coast can worry for a change. We listen to all advisories, however, it has become a habit.

Oct. 11, 10:30 A.M. Weather Bureau Advisory. SE Coast of Florida hoist storm warnings. Disturbance, Lat. 23.5 N. Long. 83.2 W. Seventy miles west north west of Havana. Travelling NNE. Bar. at Miami 29.88.

12:30 P.M. Weather Bureau Advisory. Tropical disturbance 80 miles SW of Key West. Fifty mile wind in the Dry Tortugas. Blow will pass over the Dry Tortugas and Key West sometime this afternoon. Tampa-Daytona Beach south, storm warnings. Barometer at Miami 29.81, falling. Fifty- to sixty-mile winds predicted.

We are beginning to feel rather uneasy and are keeping a close watch on the barometer as well as listening to all radio reports.

2:30 P.M. Storm intensified. Dry Tortugas, full hurricane force--100 mph reported.

4:30 P.M. Hurricane 125 miles SSW of Fort Myers. High tides. Barometer at Miami 29.75. Light rain.

Ern and I have just put up the storm shutters over the big window. It is hard work. We are soaking wet. There is no time to put up the others. We can't do it alone anyway. It is getting dark and raining hard.

6:30 P.M. Hurricane 110 miles south of Fort Myers.

Moving NNE. It looks as though we might get it. Winds at Key West, 55 mph, Miami, 38 mph. Barometer 29.69 and falling. Heavy rain. thunder and lightning. We are not enjoying our hasty dinner. The lights are flickering. They may go any minute. Damn!!

8:30 P.M. Storm midway between Key West and Everglades City. Moving about 16 mph. Barometer 29.64. Wind, east, 44 mph. Heavy rain. Severe thunderstorms.

We seem calm. We are pretending to read. We are really just waiting for the next weather advisory. We can think of nothing but the narrow shelf on which our house now stands. The ocean below us is getting very loud.

10:30 P.M. Weather Advisory. Center of small hurricane, lat. 25.5 N, long. 81.2 W. Winds 75 mph from the SW moving ENE. Miami to Vero Beach hurricane warnings! Storm moving at about 15 mph.

This is it. The wind is blowing at about 75 mph. Sheets of water driven against the windows make a tremendous racket. It is like being under a falls in a 75-mile wind. The thunder cracks and rumbles, the lightning is blinding and incessant. Here is that terrible feeling of isolation and utter helplessness again. Once more I am fighting an attack of hurricane jitters. Ern is nonchalant and sleepy--so he says! Oh, yeah!

12:30 A.M. If a weather advisory record was made, I can't find it. Anyway, the storm is still whooping it up. Torrents of rain are still being driven against the house like a million bullets. The thunder and lightning are as loud and bright and shocking as ever. Where does all the weather come from? How can it keep on and on and on?

To bed, but not to sleep. Ern is pretending to snore. He can't fool me.

2:30 A.M. No more weather reports. Storm passing out to sea. Lowest barometer reading 29.2--a mere bagatelle. It is still raining hard and blowing Great Guns, but it is relaxing a little. We are exhausted.

For eight hours the rain fell down in floods, and the thunder and lightning roared and snapped. From 12 to 15 inches of rain fell in that time. At the height of the storm 1.3 inches of rain fell in ten minutes. Our normal yearly rainfall is 60 inches. We have already had over 90 inches this year.

On Oct 17th, the Weather Bureau advised there was a disturbance SE of Turk's Island. This hurricane passed us by fortunately, but struck Bermuda on Oct. 20th. This makes four hurricanes in a month, which I think should be a record.

And so another Hurricane Season passes (we hope). South Florida has had too much water fall on it in too short a time. The Negro Sections are the worst. Typhoid shots are being given to thousands.

I insisted that Cozetta, my colored "maid" take her three pickaninnies and all get shots.

Our good friend Cap, the saltiest salt in South Florida, says the September 17th hurricane was the worst he has ever seen and Cap has sailed the seas for forty years. His barometer went down to 27.90, the lowest he has known the glass to fall. It is his opinion that we were merely brushed by the lower fringe of a monster storm. If we had been hit by all the power that hurricane packed, there would have been no one left to tell the tale. The weather planes could not fly above this storm--it was too high for them.

What little man is going to dissipate a 'cane by throwing snow balls at it?

* * *

The Woolers' experience during the 1947 hurricane season, as recorded so splendidly by Gertrude, was the basis for more civic activity by Ernest. The eternal contributor to his community, he organized the Red Cross Water Rescue and Evacuation Committee in 1948, becoming the area commander.

That year hurricanes washed out the soil under the Sea Room of the Hillsboro Club, and the north end of the Hillsboro Bridge collapsed. The state road department worked quickly, and the bridge was repaired within a month.

In 1955 Ernest Wooler became President of the Hillsboro Inlet Improvement Association, Inc. Many attempts had been made by different groups to have the U.S. Government take over the maintenance of the inlet without success. Keeping the inlet open had been done through taxation in Pompano Beach and by solicitations of contributions from individuals.

The burden of financing this project was left to a small group. As a result, a committee was formed under the name of the Hillsboro Inlet Committee. John Weir became chairman.

In August 1956, Weir presented to the state legislature a proposal for a bill creating a tax district made up of the municipalities of Hillsboro Beach, Pompano Beach, Deerfield Beach, Lauderdale-by-the Sea and Lighthouse Point.

Ernest Wooler had spent days evaluating the storm of 1947, assessing every property in Hillsboro Beach, making notes, helping each homeowner. Fifteen years later he was still trying to prompt action based on what he had observed. In a report to the town on December 15, 1962, Wooler stated:

Our section of Florida has not been hit by a

hurricane since 1947 and I have kept a constant record of our own beach since that time. Our house was sensibly built 80 feet back of the vegetation line shown by the survey pole on the attached sketch. That hurricane took away approximately 10 percent of the town: 40 feet of land at the south end and 100 feet at the north.

As Mayor, I recommended draglining sand back from the ocean between high and low tides and dumping it level with the floor of our platform, built as a gauge--20 feet above sea level and 15 feet out. Everyone agreed, so the contract was let accordingly for the three miles of beach. This worked wonders! The town regained its beach and in 14 years the land and vegetation was back within a few feet of our survey pole.

On March 8, this year, 1962, a freak storm 1,000 miles out in the Atlantic Ocean damaged almost every beach on the Eastern seaboard (see the December issue of the National Geographic Magazine). The incoming tide began lapping at our vegetation when suddenly it changed and every incoming wave deposited sand until it built up five feet more height of beach than we had had since 1947. It covered the lower steps right up to the landing. Accretion of more sand in one single tide than in the previous 14 years! This extra sand beach lasted all summer until the full moon and high tides in the middle of November, which not only took away the extra five feet of sand, but half of our lower steps.

Another storm developed off the Carolina and Georgia coasts which lasted a week. The sea was calm; no wind at all, but the tremendous ground swells tore away our remaining lower steps and undermined the landing, taking away the beach and vegetation again. But there was a north point being pushed slowly towards us by the littoral drift. It has almost reached us. We have replaced our steps and the survey pole is only showing six feet once more, i.e., the beach is nine feet above sea level at this point.

The beach comes and goes, but I still think it better to let nature take its course, rather than build sea walls and groins or even dumping the spoil from the Intracoastal Waterway on our beach when it is widened as has been suggested by the army engineers.

* * *

In 1963 Wooler was quoted as saying, "Leave the beach alone. Let nature take its course rather than build sea walls and groins or even dump rocks on the beach. In time the sand will come back." He strongly opposed the building of groins in Deerfield Beach as potentially damaging to the Hillsboro beaches.

In a letter sent from the U.S. Army Engineer District in Jacksonville, on September 18, 1962, a response to Wooler's written opposition was sent to him:

You may be assured that your remarks and the possible effects of the proposed pier and groins at Deerfield Beach upon the public rights of navigation have been given careful attention. The work is not believed to be an unreasonable obstruction to navigation and Department of the Army permits are being issued as requested.

Your interest in this matter is appreciated.

Sincerely yours,
Keith M. Hartsfield
Acting Chief
Operations Division

In a further comment on the matter Wooler stated: *"The real secret to stopping erosion in Deerfield and Pompano is to close up the Boca Inlet."* His predictions would return to haunt Hillsboro Beach.

Hurricanes acquired names during the 1940s, with the phonetic alphabet--Able, Baker, Charlie, Dog, Easy--of World War II providing the first list of names. In 1953 the weather bureau began giving hurricanes female names, such as Alice, Flossy and Donna. From 1961-93 there were 27 named storms recorded--statistically an overall reduction from previous years.

By the late 1960s the residents of Hillsboro Beach had again become concerned about their eroding beaches. Builders were asked to keep the town's sand within the town rather than hauling hundreds of truckloads across the 14th Street Bridge for fill for apartment complexes elsewhere. Citizens indicated they were willing to pay an assessment or contribution toward any long range beach erosion plan.

In 1969 there was, among other charter changes proposed to the state legislature, a bid for town power regarding erosion. As Town Attorney Russell Clarke pointed out, the one substantial power that had never been granted to the town of Hillsboro Beach had to do with beach erosion. "Although Hillsboro Beach is incorporated in the Broward County Beach Erosion District," he said, "they have received no help or assistance from Broward County and have received no return on property taxes paid to the Broward County Beach Erosion District." The reason for this, as Clarke conceded, was the fact that all the beaches in the town are private property.

Because of that reality, Hillsboro Beach proposed that the town be given the same beach erosion authority as had been created for Jupiter and Hobe Sound. Although Hillsboro Beach had not made any attempt to withdraw from the Broward County Beach Erosion District--even though they had gotten no relief from that legislation and knew they could expect none--they were asking for legislative machinery to combat beach erosion within their own town limits. The state granted the town's request.

On March 6, 1970, the Beach Erosion Advisory Committee, headed by Earle Williams, Clifton Graham and Floyd Garman, made its recommendations. They suggested that the costs be divided as follows:

1. a. Seawalls, wing back walls, back fill and engineering of these items would be assessed against the individual property owner.

1. b. Replenishment sand, nourishment sand, groin engineering, and groin maintenance would be a responsibility of the town.

1. c. Installation cost of groins would be pro-rated, on a front foot basis, among the individual property owners benefiting directly from their use.

2. Groins should be installed at approximately the same time as replenishment sand is placed--to protect the sand. The present state moratorium against groin construction will have to be lifted, but we understand that this is possible if replenishment sand is provided and nourishment sand is assured.

3. Access roads or easements from A1A for maintenance of walls, revetments, groins, and beaches should be provided at frequent intervals.

4. Lengthening of jetties of Boca Raton Inlet would seriously increase the Hillsboro Beach erosion problem. We recommend that immediate actin be taken to prevent their lengthening. Also, we have previously recommended a sand transfer plan be installed at the inlet to transfer sand south.

5. Sand replenishment and nourishment will start soon at Pompano. The parties involved should be contacted immediately with the idea that sand may be pumped on Hillsboro Beaches immediately after the work is finished at Pompano.

Attorney Clarke was authorized to draw up a resolution to hold a referendum election for an ad valorem bond issue. The referendum was expected to be ready by March 2, 1971, the date of the general election. The commission also moved to establish a new mean high water line as recommended in the report of the beach erosion committee. The plat of the mean high water base line, 5,000 feet, was executed and sent to Tallahassee.

A bond proposition was passed in the amount of $888,000 at the rate of seven percent. Out of a total of 398 voters, 288 were for the bond issue. A voluntary committee was organized to acquaint the taxpayers with the cost and other particulars of the bond issue. An integral part of the program which voters approved was periodic beach renourishment.

The bond issue was contested by the Island House, which did not wish to participate in the cost on grounds that it was not a beachfront owner. Funds set aside for erosion purposes were frozen. The courts ruled against Island House, stating that those who profit by the beach should pay to renourish it. This was construed to mean the entire town.

The city replenishment program pumped sand only to the point where the private property of the beachfront apartments began. From the mean high water mark to shore, there was a gully which was filled by residents along the beach, with the cooperation of the dredging company.

By October 2, 1972, the beach restoration project was complete.

For many years the beach renourishment measures were adequate. From time to time, however, residents reported problems. In 1979 a homeowner at the south end of town had to strategically place large bags of concrete on his property in order to protect it. Although the Hillsboro Club had renourished its beach periodically, in 1980 its manager, Norman Sheffield, reported that their beach was the best it had been in 30 years. Three years later, he reported that the property lost more sand than it had in 1947, the year of the last big hurricane.

In 1984 Deerfield Beach added rocks to the south end of their beach, and beach access was blocked. That same year, Port de Mer was experiencing severe beach erosion.

In 1990 Mayor Ann Grainger, stating that the town charter provides for a citizens Erosion Committee consisting of three members, recommended for that committee: Mrs. Jan Moran, Mr. Don Mahoney and Mr. F. Paul Kendall.

The last decade has brought fewer storms, but there was one during that period which was considered the most destructive natural disaster in U.S. history.

There had been only 14 named storms in 1990, and only two of them came to Florida. Marco slightly touched the northwest portion of Florida; Klaus got into the central and north central part of the state. In 1991 no hurricanes struck Florida.

On August 23, 1992, however, a category 4 hurricane, Andrew, struck with a vengeance. The death toll, estimated at 41, was far less than that of other hurricanes of comparable strength. Accounting in part for the low death rate were the massive evacuations that had been ordered and executed and other preparations based on early predictions and warnings. Other statistics, however, were incredible.

Just the *assessment* of the widespread destruction--including that of crops, homes and vessels--took a long time.

Bitter lessons about building and planning for hurricane protection were learned in the aftermath of Andrew, but they provided residents with knowledge that will help them survive with less property damage during the next one. Except for strong winds, Hillsboro Beach escaped once more. The town has yet to experience "the big one."

Yet Hillsboro Beach is again experiencing severe erosion pains. Should the blame be put on Andrew, on Deerfield's groins, on Boca Inlet, or just Mother Nature? In 1996 homeowner Joe Carvin, from the north end of the Mile, appeared before the commission to explain his perception of the problem. He and fellow condo owners near him had had several meetings about the issue, and he came to the commission armed with pictures of where their beach "used to be." The following month, January 1997, the commission decided to investigate and work on ways to fund a beach renourishment project.

Mayor Chuck Sussman has proceeded with the plan, working with coastal engineers and applying for programs to fund the project. The north end of town needs strong restoration; this will only be accomplished with a lot of government coordination and support from the city.

"Hopefully, we'll have the sand on the beach at the end of this year," said Mayor Sussman. "But," he added, "it will be a temporary solution to an ongoing problem."

13

Lists

Mayors and Town Commissioners

1939

(appointed)

Mayor .... J. Allen Malcolm
Commissioners .... Albert Markland
Herbert Malcolm

Beginning in 1949, officials were elected.

1949

Mayor .... Ernest Wooler
Vice Mayor .... Herbert L. Malcolm
Commissioner .... Fred Billing

1950

Mayor .... Herbert L. Malcolm
Vice Mayor .... Marie R. McCollom
Commissioner .... Ernest Wooler

1951

Mayor .... Herbert L. Malcolm
Vice Mayor .... Marie R. McCollom
Commissioner .... Benton A. Beatty

Commissioners Added
By Charter Changes 12/51 .... Elisha H. Cannon
A.D. Henderson

1952

Mayor .... G. Russell French
Vice Mayor .... Anne H. Cannon
Commissioners .... Benton A. Beatty
Marie R. McCollom
A.D. Henderson

1953

Mayor .... G. Russell French
Vice Mayor .... Anne H. Cannon
Commissioners .... Thaddeus R. Benson
Marie R. McCollom
Herbert L. Malcolm

1954

Mayor .... G. Russell French
Vice Mayor .... Thaddeus R. Benson
Commissioners .... Herbert L. Malcolm
Allan T. Burke
Marie R. McCollom

1955

Mayor .... Thaddeus R. Benson
Vice Mayor .... A.D. Henderson
Commissioners .... Allan T. Burke
G. Russell French
Nicholas O. Schlangen

1956

Mayor .... Thaddeus R. Benson
Vice Mayor .... A.D. Henderson
Commissioners .... Obie J. Smith
R.H. Galigher
Nicholas O. Schlangen

After Benson's death 3/56:
A.D. Henderson appointed Mayor
Schlangen appointed Vice Mayor
Frank F. Neaville appointed commissioner: Benson's term

1957

Mayor .... A.D. Henderson
Vice Mayor .... Obie J. Smith
Commissioners .... Allen K. Reid
Anne H. Cannon
R.H. Galigher

1958

Mayor .... A.S. Henderson
Vice Mayor .... Allen K. Reid
Commissioners .... Frank F. Neaville
Herbert L. Malcolm
Anne H. Cannon

1959

Mayor .... A.D. Henderson
Vice Mayor .... Allen K. Reid
Commissioners .... Frank F. Neaville
Clint B. K
Anne H. Cannon

1960

Mayor .... A.D. Henderson
Vice Mayor .... Anne H. Cannon
Commissioners .... Benton A. Beatty
Clint B. King
Ruth P. Markland

1961

Mayor .... A.D. Henderson
Vice Mayor .... Anne H. Cannon

Commissioners .... Ruth P. Markland
Benton A. Beatty
Clint B. King

1962

Mayor .... A.D. Henderson
Vice Mayor .... Anne H. Rode
Commissioners .... Ruth P. Markland
Baird Tewksbury
Benton A. Beatty

1963

Mayor .... A.D. Henderson
Vice Mayor .... Anne H. Rode
Commissioners: .... Ruth P. Markland
Baird Tewksbury

1964

Mayor .... A.D. Henderson
Vice Mayor .... Anne H. Rode
Commissioners: .... Benton A. Beatty
Floyd Grainger
Alma E. Tillotson

1965

Mayor .... Floyd Grainger
Vice Mayor .... Anne H. Rode
Commissioners .... Benton A. Beatty
Alma E. Tillotson
Marshall C. Sanford

1966

Mayor .... Arthur R. Wood
Vice Mayor .... Anne H. Rode
Commissioners .... Christian J. Tuuelson
Charles G. Stradella
Marshall C. Sanford

1967

Mayor .... Ann H. Rode
Vice Mayor ....Charles G. Stradella
Commissioners .... Arthur R. Wood
Marshall C. Sanford
Christian J. Truelson

1968

Mayor .... Christina J. Truelson
Vice Mayor .... Anne H. Rode
Commissioners ....Marshall C. Sanford
Charles G. Stradella
Arthur R. Wood

1969

Mayor ....Charles G. Stradella
Vice Mayor .... William R. Stuart
Commissioners .... David W. Healy
Marshall C. Sanford
Christian J. Truelson

1970

Mayor .... William R. Stuart
Vice Mayor .... John W. Erickson
Commissioners ....Marshall C. Sanford
David W. Healy
Keith M. Brooks

1971

Mayor .... John W. Erickson
Vice Mayor .... David W. Healy
Commissioners: ....Keith M. Brooks
E. Boykin Hartley
Charles G. Stradella

1972

Mayor ....Keith M. Brooks

Vice Mayor .... Charles G. Stradella

Commissioners .... Alfred T. Sheldrick
Clyde Shaffer
E. Boykin Hartley

1973

Mayor .... Keith M. Brooks

Vice Mayor .... Clyde Shaffer

Commissioners .... John W. Erickson
Alfred T. Sheldrick
Dewey A. Hagen

1974

Mayor .... Clyde C. Shaffer

Vice Mayor .... John W. Erickson

Commissioners .... Dewey A. Hagen
Alfred Housman
J. Melvin Mitchell

1975

Mayor .... Clyde C. Shaffer

Vice Mayor .... John W. Erickson

Commissioners .... Alfred Housman
Dewey A. Hagen
J. Melvin Mitchell (deceased-9/75)

1976

Mayor .... Clyde C. Shaffer

Vice Mayor .... Dewey A. Hagen

Commissioners .... Alfred Housman
John W. Erickson
Harold J. Heymann
(appointed 10/6/75 to fill Mitchell's term)

1977

Mayor .... Clyde C. Shaffer

Vice Mayor .... John W. Erickson

Commissioners .... Alfred Housman
Dewey A. Hagen
Harold J. Heymann

1978

Mayor .... John W. Erickson
Vice Mayor .... Clyde C. Shaffer
Commissioners .... Alfred Housman
Dewey A. Hagen
Harold J. Heymann

1979

Mayor .... John W. Erickson
Vice Mayor .... Alfred Housman
Commissioners .... Clyde C. Shaffer
Keith G. Cone
W. Scott Ryan

1980

Mayor .... John W. Erickson
Vice Mayor .... W. Scott Ryan
Commissioners .... Alfred Housman
Keith G. Cone
Clyde C. Shaffer
Richard McCarty
(appointed 10/6/80 to fill Shaffer's term)

1981

Mayor .... John W. Erickson
Vice Mayor .... W. Scott Ryan
Commissioners .... Keith Cone
Ann Grainger
Richard McCarty

1982

Mayor .... John W. Erickson
(resigned 3/22/83)
Vice Mayor .... W. Scott Ryan

Commissioners .... Richard McCarty
Ann Grainger
Keith G. Cone (resigned 1/83)
Andrew O'Malley (appointed to replace Cone)

1983

Mayor .... Ann Grainger

Vice Mayor .... Andrew P. O'Malley

Commissioners .... Alfred Shure
Andre LaBonte
Richard McCarty

1984

Mayor .... Ann Grainger

Vice Mayor .... Andrew P. O'Malley

Commissioners .... Richard McCarty
Andre LaBonte
Alfred Shure

1985

Mayor .... Ann Grainger

Vice Mayor .... Andrew P. O'Malley
(deceased 5/85)
Andrew Baglino

Commissioners .... Alfred Shure
Richard McCarty
Andre LaBonte (resigned 12/85)
Howard A. Spielman (appointed 12/2/85)

1986

Mayor .... Ann Grainger

Vice Mayor .... Richard McCarty

Commissioners .... Andrew Baglino
Chuck Davis
Howard Spielman (resigned 11/1/86)
Edward Jones (appointed 11/3/86 to fill Spielman's term)

1987

Mayor .... Ann Grainger
Vice Mayor .... Andrew Baglino
Commissioners .... Chuck Davis
Richard McCarty
Edward Jones

1988

Mayor .... Edward Jones
Vice Mayor .... Richard McCarty
Commissioners .... Chuck Davis
Ann Grainger
Andrew Baglino

1989

Mayor .... Ann Grainger
Vice Mayor .... Andrew Baglino
Commissioners .... Chuck Sussman
Beatrice Crouse
Richard McCarty

1990

Mayor .... Ann Grainger
Vice Mayor .... Andrew Baglino
Commissioners .... Chuck Sussman
Richard McCarty
Beatrice Crouse (resigned 11/90)
Gerald Milot (appointed to fill Crouse's term)

1991

Mayor .... Gerald Milot
Vice Mayor .... Richard McCarty
Commissioners .... Andrew Baglino
Ann Grainger
Chuck Sussman

1992

Mayor .... Gerald Milot
Vice Mayor .... Chuck Sussman
Commissioners .... Richard McCarty
Ann Grainger
Andrew Baglino (died 12/31/92)

1993

Mayor .... Howard Chuck Sussman
Vice Mayor .... Richard McCarty
Commissioners .... Ann Grainger
Marsha Milot
Constance Caloggero

1994

Mayor .... Howard Chuck Sussman
Vice Mayor .... Richard McCarty
Commissioner .... Constance Caloggero
Larry Fink
Marsha Milot

1995

Mayor .... Howard Chuck Sussman
Vice Mayor .... Richard McCarty
Commissioner .... Constance Caloggero
Larry Fink
Marsha Milot

1996

Mayor .... Howard Chuck Sussman
Vice Mayor .... Richard McCarty
Commissioner .... Constance Caloggero
Larry Fink
Marsha Milot

1997

Mayor .... Larry Fink

Vice Mayor .... Richard McCarty
Commissioners .... Howard Chuck Sussman
Marsha Milot
Constance Caloggero

Police Officers

List Courtesy of Lt. Robert H. Jones

Amo Angeletti[1]
Charles Kanode
John Garland[1]
Raymond McMullin[1,2]
Robert Sherman[1]
Edward Ong[2]
Donald Bowlby[2]
Paul Whalen
Charles Albro
Stanley Manning[2]
Gerald Cunningham
Richard Lush
James Butler
Donald Rice[3]
William Herder
William Hole[2]
James Higby[2]
James Place
Carl Parrott[3]
Ronald Leach
Franck Andre
Donald Smith
Warren Schmidt[2]
Herbert Pugmire
Ed LeViness
Ed Zaletta
Al Harrison
Paul Lauria[3]
Pete Cumo
Leo Dupree[3]
Gordon Shoppe
Donald Gibbs
Fred Frye
Garry Liccardi
Robert Weyd[4]
James Crostick
John Cologa
Cathy Heitzberg
Donna Flattery
Brenda Mirable
Joseph Von Drak
Richard Railton[3]
Chet Park
Robert Stein
Joseph Olsen[2]
Gene Forster
John Lloyd[2]
Ronald Dischert

Richard McIlwain[3]
Phil Morgan
Robert Harris[3]
John Ocheltree[3]
Tom Millwood
Glen Goll
Frank Warren[4]
John McGann[4]
Glenn Beale[4]
Daniel Hynes[4]
Jerry Smith
William Ehrnhardt[3]
Joseph Iacona
John Carlito
Deerfield lifeguard, 1 day, name unknown
Bill Davis
Dwight Smith
Thomas Johnston
Bruce Truland
Marvin Jones
1997 Police Department
Ralph W. Dunn, chief
Robert H. Jones
Richard J. Schmitt
John K. Ballard
Joseph C. Dente
Felix D. Brugnoni
Mark G. Hall
James A. Woolsey
Armando Hernandez
Thomas D. Nagy
Jay E. Szesnat
Stephen T. Kelly
Scott W. McGourty
James M. Pugliese
Joseph J. Walker
Louis Mastandrea

[1]Former chiefs
[2]Deceased
[3]Still in law enforcement
[4]Retired

Water Department

List Courtesy of Darlene Pfister

Amo Angeletti ....# to 10/10/55

Mr. Slaughter 12/05/55-3/31/56

Raymond McMullin..............................* began 4/1/56

Eugene J. Forster ....* to 10/31/70

Maydell D. Jones 3/1/71-10/10/80

Richard Nolen 12/1/80-5/20/81

Elrod Wilson 7/1/81-8/20/82

Jeffrey F. Trotta 9/13/82-5/21/87

Edwin J. Malin 6/25/87-9/14/87

Rodney Main .... began 11/19/87

#Served as town clerk, town marshal and water manager

**Served as water superintendent and town marshal*

* * *

Administrators

. Herbert L. Malcolm and Ernest Wooler acted as town clerk until the official position was established.

Dates mark beginning of terms.

3/11/47 ....Gertrude T. Wooler

4/3/50 .... Amo Angeletti (resigned 10/10/55)

10/10/55 .... Ethel E. Grant, acting town clerk
Officially appointed 3/21/56

2/11/63 .... Anne H. Rode, acting town clerk

2/12/65 .... Margaret Froedge

5/1/72 .... Reba E. Blankenship (retired 8/15/90)

8/16/90 .... Darlene J. Pfister, acting town clerk

10/8/90 .... David L. Denman

Conclusion

The first English language historian of Florida was George R. Fairbanks. In remarks made before the founding members of the Florida Historical Society nearly 140 years ago, he said: "Everything around us recalls the past and provokes an earnest desire to look into that past, to draw out its secrets, and to bring back to our own minds and memoirs the scenes and actions of the olden time; and when our day shall in its turn be numbered with the past, and others shall have succeeded us, as we now fill the places of the generation who on this spot have been born and died, it may well be that a tribute of affectionate respect and reverence may be then bestowed upon us."

A town is a living entity, with its own family, friends, and yes, even enemies. Its face can be beautiful and charming, yet on occasion it may also show a visage of sadness, frustration or dejection. Those who love and nurture their home town can make it more charming with their effort, less sad with their hope. Only by knowing well a town's shortcomings and strengths can citizens succor it in hard times, and sustain it during good times.

To that end, *Magnificent Mile* was written. May we one day have bestowed upon us, for our efforts in Hillsboro Beach, the "affectionate respect and reverence" for which historian Fairbanks hoped.

Sources

Bibliography

Adarns, Barbara. "He Doodled to a Life's Profession," *The Fort Lauderdale News* (November 27, 1961).

"Adventures of Charles Pierce in Broward County, One Hundred Years Ago, The," *Broward Legacy,* Part II (Winter/Spring 1986): 11- 36.

Allen, Kevin. "Charles Stradella, Hillsboro ex-Mayor," *The Fort Lauderdale Sun-Sentinel* (June 21, 1989).

Austin, Daniel F. "Hillsboro River," *Brovard Legacy* (Summer/Fall 1979): 26-28.

Brown, Drollene P. "There's Gold in Them Thar Boca Beaches," ***The** Boca Raton News* (September 9, 1984): 7A.

- - - . "Tracing South Florida Tropics to the Ice Age," *The Boca Raton* News (August 14, 1985): 7A.

- - - . "When Barefoot Mailman Brought Fishy Mail The Boca Raton Nevs (April 13, 1984): 7A.

Burnett, Gene N. *Florida's Past,* Vol. I. Sarasota, Florida: Pineapple Press, 1986 (219-222).

Butler, David **F.** "The Early History of Hillsboro Inlet,"

Broward Legacy (Summer/Fall 1995): 33-39.

- - - . "Early History of Pompano Beach and Fort Lauderdale." Manuscript, 1995.

Caldwell, Gunda P. *Zust Call Me Bink.* Ovation Press, 1994.

Cap's Place Menu, courtesy of Charles Kanode.

Carr, Robert S. "An Archeological Survey of Broward County, Florida: Phase Two." Manuscript, May 1993.

Casselberry, Hibbard Jr. "A Revisit to a Lightkeeper's Home," *Broward Legacy* (April 1977): 11-15.

Clairborne, J.R. "Erwin H. Haass," *The Detroit News* (June 11, 1994).

Clifford, Candace. *Inventory* of *Historic Light Stations.* Washington D.C.: National Park Service, 1994 (54).

"Cop Honored For Firefighting at Hillsboro Club," *The Boca Raton Nevs* (August 15, 1993).

Dean, James. "Shipwrecks of Broward County," *Broward Legacy* (Ninter/spring 1983): 11-26.

Dieterich, Emily Perry. "Welcome to Cap's Place," *South Florida History Nagazine* (Spring 1990).

- - - . and Jane S. Day. "Cap's Place, A Nomination to the National Register of Historic Places," Research Atlantica, Inc.

Doehring, Fred, Iver **W.** Duedall and John N. Williams. *Florida Hurricanes and Tropical Storms Z871-2993: An Historical Survey: Technica2. Paper.* Gainesville: University of Florida Press, 1994.

d'Oliveira, Steve. "Crew Hunting for Shipwrecks off Broward," *The Fort Lauderdale Sun-Sentinel* (July 4, 1996).

Doup, **Liz.** "The Dream and the Disaster," *The Fort Lauderdale Sun- Sentinel,* "Sunshine" segment (October 27, 1991).

Esse, Lauren B. Letter to Broward Historical Commission from writer in Alpharetta, Georgia (July 18, 1990).

Evans, Michael H. Personal notes, Rolls Royce Heritage Trust (1995).

"Fire Guts Landmark Restaurant, Closes Resort," *The Deerfield Beach Observer* (April 14, 1988).

"First Eighty Years, The, 1905-1985." Newsletter of Northwood School, Lake Placid, New York.

"First Phone 1910," *The Deerfield Beach Observer* (March 10, 1966).

Gannon, Michael. *Florida: A Short History.* Gainesville: The University of Florida Press, 1993.

George, Paul S. "Flamboyant Floridiana: Broward's Unique Boom Era Development," *Broward Legacy* (Summer/Fall 1992): 2-10.

"Great War—Pompano, The," *Broward Legacy* (April 19, 1918), taken from articles previously published in *The Fort Lauderdale Sentinel.*

"Hillsboro Club Notes," *The Fort Lauderdale Daily News* (January 3, 1927).

"Hillsboro Island House to Repair, Paint Bridge," *The Deerfield Beach Observer* (February 10, 1972).

Hodges, Sharon. "Mysterious Brigantine Berthed in Hillsboro's Barefoot Mailman," *The Deerfield Beach Observer* (January 8, 1976).

Hughes, Kenneth J. "History Along the Hillsboro: The Topography, the Agriculture and the People," *Broward Legacy* (Summer/Fall 1984): 7, 36-39.

Jennison, Frank. Letter to Pompano (May 1933), courtesy of Charles Kanode.

Killebrew, Laura. *Hillsboro Club,* published in Hillsboro Beach.

"Lighthouse Service," Washington D.C.: Department of Commerce and Labor, 1911.

McIver, Stuart. "The Barefoot Mailman a Famous Local Legend," *Broward Legacy* (July 1977): 23-27.

- - - . *Glimpses* of *South Florida History.* Florida Flair Books, 1988 (45, 94, 175).

Menning, Rick. "Attorney Blasts County Over Gradual Takeover of Municipal Government," *The Deerfield Beach Observer* (June 10, 1976).

Metts, Stephen L. "The History of the United States Coast Guard Light Station at Hillsboro Inlet." Manuscript, 1996.

Office of the Light-House Board. Washington D.C.: U.S. Treasury Department, 1889.

Page, C. Clinton. "Long in Light Service: Captain Thomas Knight," *Brovard Legacy* (Ninter/Spring 1982): 27-31.

Patton, Carolyn. "Hidden Pleasures," *The Fort Lauderdale Sun- Sentinel* (October 23, 1994).

Raymond, Bill. "The Shipwreck of the Gil Blas," *Broward Legacy* (Winter/Spring 1984): 15-25.

Santaniello, **Neil.** "Hillsboro vs. Broward," *The Fort Lauderdale Sun-Sentinel.* (February 9, 1983).

Schenker, Jennifer L. "Old Guard—Town Changes Face, But Not Character," *The Fort Lauderdale Sun-Sentinel* (February 10, 1982).

"Sewer Line Construction Starts," *The Deerfield Beach Observer* (January 10, 1974).

Stewart, N. William. "Some of the Historic Circumstances That Led to the Founding of the River View Club." Speech presented to the Estahakee Chapter of the Daughters of the American Revolution (October 11, 1991).

"Town Wants Fire Equipment," *The Deerfield Beach Observer* (September 11, 1969).

Weakley, Jim, ed. *Encyclopedia of Florida.* Somerset, 1964.

Weaver, Jay. "Cap's Place Dishes Up Fresh Seafood and History," *The Fort Lauderdale Sun-Sentinel* (July 24, 1994).

Weber, Carol. "The Battle of Cap's Place," *Tropic* (March 11, 1973).

Weeks, Marilyn. "Hillsboro to Change Land Plan," *The Fort Lauderdale Sun-Sentinel* (January 16, 1989).

Wills, Charles A. A *Historical Album* of *Florida*. Brookfield, Connecticut: Millbrook Press, 1994.

Wilson, Judy. "A1A Nidening Begins This Month," *The Deerfield Beach Observer* (July 28, 1994).

- - - . "Cities Honor Their Finest. Dunn: Three Decades of Keeping Peace on the Mile," *The Deerfield Beach Observer* (Narch 9, 1995).

- - - . "Officials Seek Bike Path Opinions," *The Deerfield Beach Observer* (November 4, 1993).

- - - . "Riverview will Remain Shuttered This Season," *The DeerfieEd Beach Observer* (November 30, 1995).

Wooler, Ernest. "Reminiscences of Cooke Street," personal notes, 1964

- - - . and Gertrude Nooler. Christmas card 1947.

Zannoni, Frances Pala. "Keeping Old Florida Alive," *The Fort Lauderdale Sun-Sentinel* (September 1, 1996).

Obituary Notices

Courtesy of Kraeer Funeral Home

Interviews

Conducted by the Author

Amo Angeletti, April 1994

Betty Bateman, February and March 1997

Barbara Bittner, April 1996

Joe Carvin, June 1996

Charles Kanode, April 1996

Dean and Ann Lindstrom, March 1994

Patricia Malcolm Scott, August 1993

Mr. Firestone, Director of Development, Northwood School, Lake Placid, New York, July 1994

M. Sullivan, Lake Placid, New York, Historian, July 1994

Allen Malcolm, June 1995

James French, May 1997

Jacki O'Hara, May 1997

Susan Sampler, May 1997

Elizabeth Shaffer, March 1997